Men-at-Arms • 483

Cumberland's Culloden Army 1745–46

Stuart Reid • Illustrated by Gerry & Sam Embleton

Series editor Martin Windrow

First published in Great Britain in 2012 by Osprey Publishing,
Midland House, West Way, Botley, Oxford, OX2 0PH, UK
43-01 21st Street, Suite 220B, Long Island City, NY 11101, USA
E-mail: info@ospreypublishing.com

OSPREY PUBLISHING IS PART OF THE OSPREY GROUP

A CIP catalogue record for this book is available from the British Library

Print ISBN: 978 1 84908 846 6
PDF ebook ISBN: 978 1 84908 847 3
ePub ebook ISBN: 978 1 78200 305 2

Editor: Martin Windrow
Page layout by: Ken Vail Graphic Design, Cambridge, England
Index by Rob Munro
Map by The Map Studio
Typeset in Helvetica Neue and ITC New Baskerville
Originated by PDQ Media, Bungay, UK
Printed in China through Worldprint Ltd.

13 14 15 10 9 8 7 6 5 4 3 2

Osprey Publishing is supporting the Woodland Trust, the UK's leading
woodland conservation charity, by funding the dedication of trees.

www.ospreypublishing.com

Acknowledgements

Thanks are due to Dr. John Houlding for identifying the Marine regiment in
which Captain John Gore was serving in 1746; and to Andrew Cormack for
very kindly providing copies of his photographs of the surviving grenadier caps
belonging to Harcourt's and Granby's Regiments, and giving his consent to
reproduce them.

Author's note

In the 18th century, Argyll was generally spelled 'Argyle', and for the avoidance
of confusion this original spelling is used throughout. The county is now part of
Highland Region.
Illustrations not specifically credited otherwise are from the author's collection,
including the author's facsimile drawings from contemporary originals.

Artist's note

Readers may care to note that the original paintings from which the colour
plates in this book were prepared are available for private sale. All reproduction
copyright whatsoever is retained by the Publishers. All enquiries should be
addressed to:

www.gerryembleton.com

The Publishers regret that they can enter into no correspondence upon this
matter.

CUMBERLAND'S CULLODEN ARMY 1745–46

INTRODUCTION

The story of the last Jacobite Rising in 1745 and 1746 has traditionally been told from the viewpoint of the Highland army which so spectacularly defeated Sir John Cope at Prestonpans, marched on London only to turn back at Derby, and was eventually destroyed on Culloden Moor. Surprisingly little attention has been paid to the army that eventually defeated it there. Indeed, it is still common to find that army referred to as the 'Hanoverian' army – despite the fact that rather fewer than 20 German and Austrian soldiers, belonging to the Duke of Cumberland's personal bodyguard of hussars, actually fought at Culloden. Admittedly, at other times during the campaign there were also considerable numbers of Dutch, Swiss and Hessian soldiers (and even a Creek warrior from North America) to supplement a variety of locally raised provincial and militia units. Nevertheless, the core of the Duke of Cumberland's army throughout the Rising was composed of regular soldiers recruited from all three kingdoms of the British Isles. It was not a Hanoverian army at all, but the British Army.

A central aspect of the events of 1745 was that when the Stuart pretender Prince Charles Edward raised his standard at Glenfinnan on 19 August 1745, the response of the commander-in-chief in Britain – the elderly and ailing Field Marshal George Wade – was constrained by the fact that most of that army was actually deployed in Flanders, serving as part of a coalition of forces ranged against those of Louis XV's France. Consequently the troops immediately available in Scotland to counter the insurgency did not amount to very much, as Gen Sir John Cope afterwards recalled:

As much as I can remember on the 2nd of July the troops in Scotland were quartered thus:
Gardiner's Dragoons at Stirling, Linlithgow, Musselburgh, Kelso and Coldstream.
Hamilton's Dragoons at Haddington, Duns and the adjacent places.
N.B. – both regiments at Grass
Guise's Regiment of foot at Aberdeen, and the Coast-Quarters.
Five companies of Lee's at Dumfries, Stranraer, Glasgow and Stirling.
Murray's in the Highland Barracks. Lascelles' at Edinburgh and Leith.
Two Additional Companies of the Royals at Perth.
Two Do. of the Scottish Fuziliers at Glasgow.
Two Do. of Lord Sempill's at Cupar in Fife.
Three Do. of Lord John Murray's Highland Regiment at Crieff.
Lord Loudoun's Regiment was beginning to be raised; and besides these, there were the standing garrisons of Invalids in the castles.

His Royal Highness William Augustus, Duke of Cumberland, the second son of King George II. He was only 24 years old at the outbreak of the Rising in August 1745, but portraits show him as a portly figure, due to the long-term effects of an unhealed leg wound suffered at the battle of Dettingen in 1743. (Ann S.K. Brown Military Collection, Brown University)

Detail from Bowles' well-known print of the battle of Culloden, depicting a blue-coated staff officer and dragoon orderlies.

In thus enumerating his command, Cope followed the then common convention of referring to units by the names of their commanding officers – a practice ripe for confusion, as those concerned were transferred to other regiments or, indeed, translated to glory. The 'Murray's' that Cope listed as quartered in the Highland Barracks was Thomas Murray's 57th Foot; this had no connection at all with the three companies of Lord John Murray's 43rd Highland Regiment at Crieff. Just two months earlier the latter had been commanded by, and named after, that same Lord Sempill whose Additional Companies of the 25th Regiment now lay at Cupar.

Indeed, during the campaign there would be several changes in regimental designation. For example, Gardiner's Dragoons became Francis Ligonier's following the former's death at Prestonpans, and then Naizon's after Ligonier in turn succumbed to pleurisy in February 1746. Conversely, although Ligonier's regiment of Foot then passed to Henry Conway, and that of Monro (killed at Falkirk) passed to Louis Dejean, both regiments are generally referred to by the names of their previous commanders in most accounts of Culloden.

In recognition of this problem, fixed numbers corresponding to their seniority in the Army List had in fact been allocated to regiments at the beginning of the 1740s, appearing for the first time in the *Cloathing Book* of 1742, and were thereafter directed to be placed on regimental colours in 1743. The change was at first unpopular, and general acceptance took some time, but for the sake of clarity the regimental numbers as in use at that time are employed throughout this text. (For example, the Black Watch was then numbered as the 43rd rather than the 42nd Foot.) In case of any confusion, readers should consult the tables of regiments on pages 35–38 of this book.

CHRONOLOGY

1740

22 March   Highland companies ordered to be regimented as 43rd Foot, backdated on establishment to 25 October 1739.

1743

17 May   43rd Highlanders mutiny at Finchley.

1744

26 June   Two Additional Companies are added to establishment of each regiment then serving in Flanders, to serve as a depot.

5 July   6th Foot ordered from Warwickshire to Scotland.

1745

11 May   Battle of Fontenoy; British and allied forces defeated by French.

9 June   Allied garrison in Tournai surrenders.

19 June   Letters of service are issued for raising of Loudoun's 64th Highlanders.

5 July   Prince Charles Edward Stuart sails from France for Scotland.

19 August   Jacobite standard raised at Glenfinnan.

20 August   Gen Sir John Cope marches north from Stirling with 43rd Highlanders (2 companies), 55th Foot (5 coys) and 57th Foot, followed the next day by 58th Foot (8 coys).
Garrisons left behind, exclusive of Invalids, are: Glasgow, 21st Foot (2 coys); Stirling, 25th Foot (2 coys) and 13th Dragoons; Edinburgh, 58th Foot (2 coys) and 14th Dragoons. (Berwick, lying just south of the English border, was not part of Gen Cope's command, but was garrisoned by the other 5 companies of the 55th Foot.)

26 August   Ostend surrenders to the French; garrison includes provisional battalion of Footguards, 12th Foot and 21st Fusiliers.

29 August   Sgt Molloy, with 12 men, successfully holds Ruthven Barracks against Jacobite attack.

8 September   Additional Companies stationed in England are ordered to be formed into three provisional battalions under Marine officers.

9 September   Letters of service are issued for Edinburgh Regiment (provincials).

18 September   Jacobites seize Edinburgh.

19 September   Five companies of Blakeney's 27th Foot are ordered to Chester.

20 September   Seven Dutch battalions from the paroled garrison of Tournai arrive in the Thames.

21 September   Battle of Prestonpans; Jacobites defeat Cope's force – 6th

Front Ranks push your Bayonets 3 times 6 Mo.

This rather crude illustration from Maj George Grant's *New Highland Military Discipline* of 1757 usefully demonstrates the bayonet drill employed in the 1740s, which itself was still heavily influenced by the pike drill practiced in the 17th century.

Foot (2 coys); 43rd Highlanders (1 coy); 55th Foot (5 coys); 57th Foot; 58th Foot (8 coys); 64th Highlanders (3½ coys); 13th Dragoons; 14th Dragoons.

25 September   Units arriving in the Thames on return from Flanders – Footguards, plus 11th, 13th, 19th, 28th Foot, 32nd Fusiliers, 33rd and 34th Foot, totalling 245 officers and 7,269 rank-and-file.

27 September   The 3rd, 4th, 8th, 14th, 36th, 37th, and 59th Foot are recalled from Flanders, being ordered to embark for Newcastle upon Tyne; Provisional battalion of Footguards (ex-Ostend garrison) recalled to London.

4 October   Letters of service are issued for 15 provincial regiments already being raised in England.

10 October   The first provincial regiments are reported 'half compleat' and ready to be taken into the Line.

13 October   Convoy carrying troops originally ordered to Newcastle on 27 September finally clears Helvoetensluys, but is scattered by a gale on 18 October. Most arrive in the Tyne two days later, others at Berwick.

22 October   Final contingent embarked from Flanders – 1/1st

Edinburgh Castle as seen from the Grassmarket, illustrating the way in which this important garrison dominated the city.

6

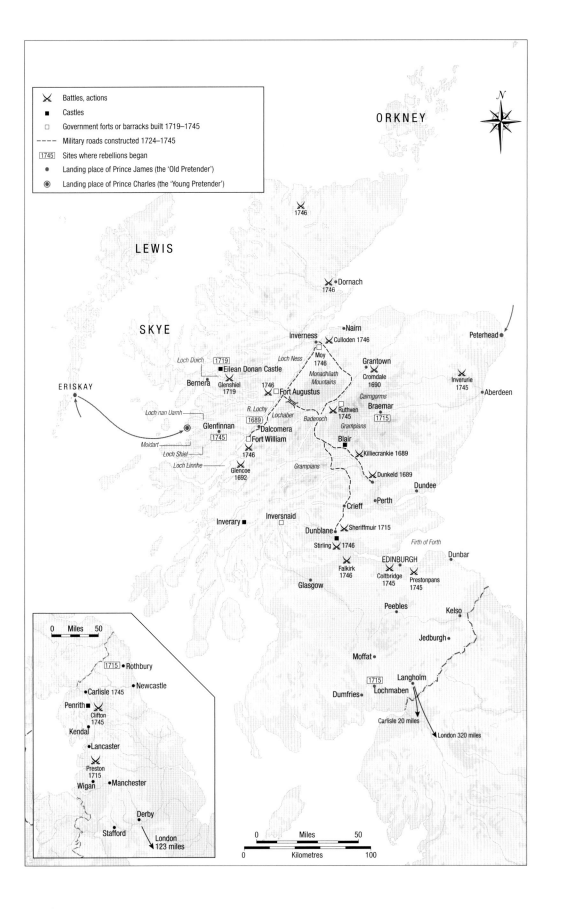

Legend:

- ✗ Battles, actions
- ■ Castles
- □ Government forts or barracks built 1719–1745
- - - - Military roads constructed 1724–1745
- 1745 Sites where rebellions began
- ● Landing place of Prince James (the 'Old Pretender')
- ◉ Landing place of Prince Charles (the 'Young Pretender')

ORKNEY

LEWIS

SKYE

ERISKAY

✗ 1746

✗ Dornach
1746

• Nairn

Inverness ✗ Culloden 1746

Loch Duich   1719
■ Eilean Donan Castle
Bernera   Glenshiel   1719
1719

Moy
1746

Loch Ness

Monadhliath
Mountains

Grantown
✗
Cromdale
1690

✗ Inverurie
1745

Loch nan Uamh

Moidart

◉ Glenfinnan
1745

1746 □ Fort Augustus

R. Lochy   1689
Lochaber   Loch Lochy   Badenoch

Cairngorms

Braemar
□
Ruthven
1745   Grampians   1715

• Aberdeen

Peterhead •

Loch Shiel

Loch Linnhe

Dalcomera
□ Fort William
1746

Glencoe
1692

Blair
■   ✗ Killiecrankie 1689

✗ Dunkeld 1689

• Dundee

Grampians

• Crieff   • Perth

Inverary ■   Inversnaid
□

Dunblane ■   ✗ Sheriffmuir 1715

Stirling ✗ 1746

Firth of Forth

• Dunbar

EDINBURGH
✗
Falkirk   Coltbridge   Prestonpans
1746   1745   1745

• Glasgow

• Peebles   • Kelso

• Jedburgh

• Moffat

1715 Langholm
• Dumfries   Lochmaben

Carlisle 20 miles

London 320 miles

Inset map (Scotland/England border):

0   Miles   50

1715 • Rothbury

• Carlisle 1745   • Newcastle

Penrith ■ ✗
Clifton
1745

Kendal •

• Lancaster

✗
Preston
1715

Wigan •   • Manchester

• Derby
London
123 miles

Stafford •

0   Miles   50

0   Kilometres   100

1 November *Marshal Wade's forces assembling at or near Newcastle upon Tyne:* 2/1st (Royals), 3rd, 4th, 8th, 13th, 14th, 27th, 34th, 36th, 37th, 59th and 62nd Foot, and Frazer's Provisional Battalion. Dutch regiments Hirzel (3 bns), Villattes (2 bns), Holstein-Gottorp (2 bns), Tissot van Patot (2 bns) and La Rocque (1 bn).
En route: 3rd Horse, 8th Dragoons, Georgia Rangers (2 troops), and Yorkshire Hunters.
At Berwick: 55th Foot (5 coys), Dutch regt La Rocque (1 bn); 13th and 14th Dragoons.

9 November Order to issue 'camp necessaries' to Provincial regiments.

14 November Carlisle surrenders to the Jacobites. 39th Foot ordered from Portsmouth to London. LtGen Roger Handasyde re-occupies Edinburgh with 14th and 59th Foot, 13th and 14th Dragoons.

19 November Col Graham's Liverpool Volunteers are ordered to Warrington, and authorized to fall back on Chester.

20 November Edinburgh Regiment reconstituted, first under Gen Handasyde, then Lord Hopetoun.

24 November The first French troops land in Scotland; the Dutch units are required to withdraw.

27 November 39th Foot ordered to Deptford.

29 November The Jacobites enter Manchester.

6 December The Jacobites begin their retreat from Derby.

(?) December *Units in and around London:* Three troops of Horse Guards and Horse Grenadier Guards (779 strong); seven battalions of Footguards (4,196); 8th Horse (4 troops), 3rd Dragoons, 10th Dragoons, 11th Dragoons.
Dartford Heath: 11th, 19th, 28th, 30th Foot, 32nd Fusiliers, 33rd and 39th Foot (4,900).
Abingdon and Aylesbury 1/1st (Royals); *Hertford and Ware* 23rd Fusiliers; *Guildford* 31st Foot (total, 1,600).

18 December Action at Clifton: 3rd, 10th and 11th Dragoons; Cumberland's Hussars (1 troop); Georgia Rangers (2 troops); Yorkshire Hunters.

23 December Highland Independent Companies (7 in total) under

Ruthven Barracks, Kingussie, was typical of the patrol bases established by Gen Wade in the Highlands before the Rising. In August 1745, Sgt Terry Molloy and a garrison of a dozen men successfully defended it against several hundred Highlanders, but surrendered in the following year when threatened with artillery fire. The barracks were then burned, but nevertheless remained in use for some time afterwards by the Highland Independent Companies.

MacLeod and Culcairn defeated by Jacobites at Inverurie near Aberdeen.

30 December The Jacobites surrender Carlisle to Duke of Cumberland (besieging army as 5 January return below).

1746

5 January *Units in and around London:* Horse Guards, Horse Grenadier Guards, 8th Horse (2 troops), 1st (Royal) Dragoons, 4th Dragoons, Footguards, 1/1st (Royals), 11th, 12th, 16th, 18th, 19th Foot, 23rd Fusiliers, 28th, 30th Foot (less 2 coys on Jersey), 31st Foot, 32nd Fusiliers, 33rd, 39th Foot (less 2 coys on Guernsey), 43rd Highlanders.
Bristol 24th and 72nd Foot; *Chester* 73rd and 77th Foot; *Cornwall* 75th and 79th Foot; *Dover* 15th Foot; *Harwich (& Landguard Fort)* 76th Foot; *Hull* 70th Foot; *Portsmouth* 67th Foot; *Shrewsbury* 78th Foot.
With Duke of Cumberland: 8th Horse (less 2 troops), 9th and 10th Horse; 3rd and 10th Dragoons; 14th Foot, 21st Fusiliers, 25th, 68th, 69th, 71st and 74th Foot.
With Wade and Hawley: 3rd and 4th Horse, 8th Dragoons, 2/1st (Royals), 3rd, 4th, 8th, 13th, 14th, 27th, 34th, 36th, 38th, 59th and 62nd Foot; Dutch battalions.
In Scotland: 6th, 55th, 57th and 58th Foot, 64th Highlanders; and unbrigaded Additional Companies of 1st (Royals), 21st Fusiliers, 25th Foot and 43rd Highlanders.

Robert Gordon's College, Aberdeen. The recently completed central block of the school, seen here, was palisaded around and served as a substantial fort for the garrison established in the burgh by the Duke of Cumberland. For the two weeks before Culloden an Aberdeen headquarters for the duke and his second-in-command Gen Henry Hawley were established in Provost Skene's house nearby, which also survives.

17 January Battle of Falkirk; Jacobites defeat Hawley's force – 2/1st (Royals), 3rd, 4th, 8th, 13th, 14th, 27th, 34th, 36th, 37th Foot, 42nd Highlanders (1 coy), 59th, 62nd Foot, 64th Highlanders (3 coys); Edinburgh Regiment (detachment), Argyleshire Men (12 coys), Glasgow Volunteers, Paisley Volunteers, Stirling Volunteers (1 coy?); 10th, 13th and 14th Dragoons.

1 February The Jacobites withdraw northwards.

8 February Hessian units land at Leith: regiments Garde (833 strong), Prinz Maximilian (829), Ansbach (836), Von Donop (833), Prinz Friedrich Wilhelm (907); consolidated Grenadier regiment (830), and Hussars (98).

16 February Loudoun's abortive raid on Moy – 43rd and 64th Highlanders (1 coy each) and Highland Independent Companies.

18 February Jacobites capture Inverness – 6th Foot (1 coy), Independent Coys (2).

22 February British army enters Aberdeen.

5 March Fort Augustus surrenders to Jacobites – 6th Foot (3 coys).

9

17 March	30th Foot ordered to Cape Breton, Nova Scotia.
20 March	Jacobite raid on Keith – Argyleshire Men (70), 10th Horse (31). Jacobite siege of Fort William begins – 6th Foot (2 coys), Highland Independent Company.
22 March	12th, 16th, 18th and 24th Foot ordered to Scotland by sea.
26 March	French gold shipment captured at Tongue – 64th Highlanders (1 coy) and Highland Independent Company.
1 April	Jacobites abandon the siege of Fort William.
8 April	Cumberland's army marches from Aberdeen.
12 April	British army crosses River Spey.
15 April	Cromartie's Jacobites are ambushed and captured at Dunrobin by three Highland companies.
16 April	Battle of Culloden; defeat of Jacobites by Cumberland's army – 2/1st (Royals), 3rd, 4th, 8th, 13th, 14th, 20th, 21st, 25th, 27th, 34th, 36th, 37th Foot, 43rd Highlanders (1 coy), 59th, 62nd Foot, 64th Highlanders (3 coys), Argyle Companies (4 coys), 10th Horse, 10th and 11th Dragoons, Cumberland's Hussars.
24 April	57th and 58th Foot ordered to be drafted to complete regiments earmarked for L'Orient expedition.
20 May	Hessian contingent are ordered to embark for home from Newcastle upon Tyne.
10 June	The Provincial regiments are ordered to be disbanded, with temporary exception of 68th, 69th, 71st and 74th Foot still guarding rebel prisoners.
15 September	10th (Kingston's) Horse disbanded, but reconstituted as 15th Dragoons.
14 December	3rd and 4th Troops of Horse Guards reduced; 2nd, 3rd and 4th Horse to become Dragoons (1st–3rd Dragoon Guards from 10 Jan 1747); 5th–8th Horse become 1st–4th Irish Horse.

Another detail from Bowles' print of Culloden. Under magnification, it shows all the British regulars with their coat skirts unhooked.

ORGANIZATION

Regiments

At the core of the British Army were the 69 red-coated regular infantry regiments. Each of them, with the exception of the Footguards and the 1st (Royal) Regiment, was organized as a single battalion, which normally comprised ten companies including one of grenadiers. The Royals had two battalions, but as they rarely if ever served together they were to all intents and purposes independent units. The three regiments of Footguards had a unique organization all of their own. Being much larger than normal infantry regiments – with 24 companies in the 1st Footguards, and 16 apiece in the Coldstreamers and Scots Guards – they were in the habit of forming *ad hoc* battalions for service as and when required. While such provisional battalions were usually formed of companies drawn from a single regiment, this was not invariably the case, and the battalion at Ostend (see Chronology, 26 August 1745) was formed from drafts from all three regiments.

Although it sometimes varied, each company had a notional strength of 70 rank-and-file (71 in the Footguards), so a battalion had 700 men. In fact, the difficulty of maintaining companies at this strength in wartime is illustrated by the range of unit strengths at Culloden: the strongest infantry battalion, Monro's 37th, mustered 426 men, while the weakest, Blakeney's 27th, had just 300 – less than half of its theoretical establishment. Only the grenadier company in each regiment was maintained at something like its proper strength, by constantly milking the battalion companies or 'hat men' of their most experienced soldiers.

Contrary to popular belief, the grenadier companies were not automatically formed from the tallest men; according to the Duke of Cumberland's own orders, they were 'to be completed out of the best Men of their respective Regiments, and to be constantly kept so'. The reason for this was that when the battalion was formed in a battle line the grenadiers were split into two platoons, with one deployed to guard each flank. At least they still remained with their own battalions; there are no instances during the 1745–46 campaign of the pernicious practice of culling grenadier companies from their parent units to form consolidated elite battalions, as was to be so common during the Seven Years' War and the American Revolution. The cavalry equivalent to the company of Foot was the troop, with a notional strength of 59 men. Normally there were six troops to a regiment, although the Royal Horse Guards (Blues) and the 2nd Horse both had nine, while the Life Guards had a hybrid organization, with four troops of horse and two of dragoons. In the very early days dragoon regiments, as mounted infantry, had had one of their troops designated as grenadiers; but the practice had ceased by this period, except in so far as the superior status of the two troops of dragoons forming part of the Household Cavalry was marked by their designation as Horse Grenadier Guards.

The uniform worn by this 'hat man' of a battalion company of Cholmondley's 34th Regiment of Foot, illustrated in a watercolour from the 1742 *Cloathing Book*, had probably not altered to any significant degree before the outbreak of the Jacobite Rising three years later. See below under 'The Regiments' for facing colours.

Officers

In either case, the company or troop was commanded by a captain, who might also be a field officer, since all three of these – the regimental colonel, the lieutenant-colonel and the major – each commanded a company of his own. The captains were in turn seconded by lieutenants, dignified in the case of the colonel's company by the hybrid title of captain-lieutenant, in recognition of the fact that he was the *de facto* company commander. The grenadier company always boasted two lieutenants, since it was normally divided in two and posted on either flank of the battalion. In wartime an additional lieutenant was temporarily added to the establishment of each of the other companies as well, in order to allow for the inevitable casualties. Finally, with the

William Hogarth's famous representation of the Footguards' march to Finchley in 1745. Under close examination it provides an extraordinary wealth of detail – not least, the woman (right) with both an infant and a slung firelock on her back. The fifer next to the drummer (far right) is clearly a young boy.

exception of the grenadiers, each company also boasted a junior subaltern. Usually designated as an ensign in infantry regiments and as a cornet in the cavalry, or in fusilier and marine regiments as a second lieutenant, he was in effect an apprentice officer.

Regimental staff

At a higher level regiments were notionally commanded by a colonel. Although such gentlemen were frequently employed elsewhere as general officers or on particular service, in the 1740s it was far from unknown for them still to be found actually leading their regiments into battle – and, like the unfortunate Col Gardiner of the 13th Dragoons, to be killed doing so. More commonly, however, regiments were commanded on a day-to-day basis by one or both of the other 'field officers', the lieutenant-colonel or the major. He was assisted by the adjutant, who answered directly to the major and was responsible for ordinary administrative and disciplinary matters. It was not unknown to find officers, usually promoted former NCOs, solely employed as adjutants, but normally they had to juggle their regimental duties with those of their parent company. Otherwise, the regimental staff (exclusive of any rankers acting as clerks) comprised the chaplain, who was to all intents and purposes a mythical being, never seen at headquarters; and the surgeon, who was accounted equal to a captain when it came to the allocation of quarters, but was not otherwise regarded as a military man unless he had also purchased a commission as a company officer.

Technical branches

The Royal Artillery was organized quite differently, due to the fact that it was for most practical purposes a quite separate service, whose officers' first allegiance was to the Board of Ordnance, just as Royal Navy officers answered to the Board of Admiralty. Outwardly the rank structure was similar but, as with the Footguards, there was no fixed battalion organization at this stage. The basic unit remained the company, commanded by a captain or captain-lieutenant, while more senior officers

The Life Guards, as befitting their status, had a unique style of uniform displaying a profusion of gold lace, as seen in this illustration from the *Cloathing Book.* The horse furniture is basically red trimmed with gold, and the rolled cloak blue.

generally served on the staff. At Culloden the senior Royal Artillery officer, Maj William Belford, occupied a staff position as the Duke of Cumberland's Commander Royal Artillery (CRA), while the junior officers and the 95 gunners and 'matrosses' (unskilled gun crew) all belonged to Capt-Lt John Godwin's company. A major problem earlier in the campaign had been a shortage of actual gunners. Thus at Prestonpans, Cope's CRA Maj Eaglesfield Griffith found himself having to serve the guns himself with the aid of four Invalids, nine borrowed sea gunners (who promptly ran away), and the ever-versatile LtCol Charles Whitefoord of the 5th Marines.

Such flexibility and improvisation were not uncommon, and although certain individuals no doubt established a reputation for their skill in a particular aspect of the art and science of gunnery, generally speaking artillerymen were expected to do their best with whatever tools they were given at a particular time. For the Culloden campaign Capt Godwin's men were assigned ten small 3-pounder cannon and six mortars, as being best suited for travelling over the rough countryside and poor roads to be expected in the north of Scotland. However, these guns did not 'belong' to the company; when Godwin's company was rotated out they went into store at Edinburgh Castle, ready to be used by the next company assigned to serve in Scotland.

It was a similar story with the engineers. In 1716 a corps of Engineers had been formed comprising 3 Directors, 6 Engineers in Ordinary, 6 Engineers Extraordinary, 6 Sub-Engineers and 6 Practitioner Engineers, but no workmen. All of them, as their titles suggest, were essentially technical advisors, and it was a source of some unhappiness to them that, unlike their colleagues in the Royal Artillery, they did not actually hold military rank – and would not do so until 14 May 1757. Until then it was not uncommon to find engineer officers purchasing or otherwise acquiring commissions in regiments of the Line, both to supplement their pay and to cement their military status. Quite typically, Capt Alexander Grossett, who was murdered by a rebel prisoner while serving as an engineer on Cumberland's staff at Culloden, was also a captain in Price's 14th Foot.

LEADERSHIP & RECRUITMENT – THE LINE

Regimental officers

There is still a strong presumption that those who led the Army were wealthy aristocrats, or at least belonged to the landed gentry; but closer examination of the 18th century officer corps reveals that only some 24 per cent bore inherited titles or were the younger sons of noblemen, while a further 16 per cent came from the untitled landed gentry. Moreover, the distribution of these gentlemen was very uneven, with the majority to be found in the Guards and regiments of Horse. In ordinary regiments of the Line the greater majority of officers – like the unfortunate Capt Grossett of the 14th – were found amongst the sons of middle-class professionals and merchants (Grossett's brother, Walter, was a customs officer, and the government's spymaster in Scotland). There was also a small and close-knit body of families with a tradition of military service, whose influence on the development of the Army was out of all proportion to their number.

As with any profession at this time, securing a place required some form of investment. The money normally paid to purchase a commission served both as a bond for an officer's good behaviour during his service, and as the interest-bearing capital which provided his annual pay. As most officers were actually far from wealthy, finding the money with which to purchase each step of promotion in their career was therefore a serious challenge. It almost invariably required substantial family or bankers' loans, precariously repaid by subventions from their personal pay, dividends, perquisites and occasional prize money.

Promotion was also a protracted process. In theory it was sometimes possible for a wealthy individual to purchase his way to the top within a matter of weeks, but this was actually exceptional. Both Kings George I and George II, and the Duke of Cumberland, took a genuine interest in the Army and the fitness and competence of those who officered it. In 1740 it took an officer an average of 19 years from entering the Army to gaining command of an infantry company, and a scarcely less glacial 17 years to reach command of a cavalry troop. The good fortune of a 'bloody war and a sickly season' did of course speed things up somewhat, as did the 'interest' of influential superiors, but by the end of that decade it was still taking an average of ten years to attain a captaincy.

The process of promotion could also be accomplished by 'raising for rank', when an increase in the military establishment provided the opportunity for an ambitious officer to gain a step in promotion by recruiting a certain quota of men largely at his own expense. Usually this was done by obtaining leave to raise or assist in the raising of an Independent Company. When complete, the recruits would then be transferred into a regiment of the Line and the officers placed on half-pay until such time as they could effect an exchange at their new rank into their old regiment, or even a different one. Sometimes whole regiments might be raised in this way, as strikingly evidenced by what were referred to as the 'Noblemens' Regiments', discussed below.

Conversely, on his retirement an officer was normally expected to

Colonel James Gardiner of the 13th Dragoons, here in an engraving from the *New Christian Magazine* in 1784, lived in a house named Olive Stobb on what became the battlefield of Prestonpans. Fatally wounded in the battle of 21 September 1745, he died on a mattress laid out in his own garden. Command of his regiment passed to Francis Ligonier, who himself died in February 1746, when it was taken over by Col Naizon. (Incidentally, Gardiner's house has recently been restored.)

provide for himself by selling his commissions and re-investing the proceeds in an annuity. If his regiment had been disbanded, however – as periodically occurred on the happy outbreak of peace – he would obviously be unable to find a buyer. So, instead of being removed entirely from the Army List, surplus units were 'reduced' to comprise just the officers alone, who were then entitled to draw half-pay – or to exchange with officers in standing regiments who did wish to retire but were for one reason or another unable to 'sell out'. The corollary to this was that officers on the half-pay list were expected to actively seek employment in any new corps that might subsequently be raised, and as an inducement to do so they could normally expect to receive a step up in rank when they did.

Recruitment

With certain very clearly defined exceptions, enlistment into the ranks of the Army was voluntary. Recruiting was almost invariably carried out by small parties of officers, NCOs and drummers in possession of a 'beating order', which literally authorized them to beat a drum within a specified locality, and to invite volunteers to step forward in response to whatever blandishments they might offer.

This was straightforward enough if a battalion was serving at home, and was able deploy a number of recruiting parties around the districts in which it was quartered. An interesting consequence of this in 1745 was that well over half of Gen Cope's officers and men at Prestonpans were actually Scots; the principal exceptions were his two regiments of dragoons, which came from Ireland, and the 6th Foot, which had been brought up to strength in Warwickshire before being posted to Scotland.

Gunner, Royal Artillery, after a 1742 watercolour. By 1748 a considerable amount of yellow lace was being worn on the uniform, but it is unclear whether this had been introduced after this watercolour was painted, or whether this image depicts a plain working uniform. See commentaries to Plates C1 and C2.

The Duke of Argyle rather uncharitably claimed in 1740 that those recruited into the Army were for the most part 'too stupid or too infamous to learn or carry on a Trade', but the reality was that at this period most of those enlisting were agricultural labourers or weavers laid off after the harvest or during one of the periodic slumps in trade. For that reason recruiting parties, rather than relying upon enlisting chance-met individuals on the road, were normally to be found at fairs and markets, and particularly at the periodic agricultural hiring or 'feeing' fairs where large numbers of men could be found looking for work.

When being attested, a prospective recruit was required to declare under oath that he was a Protestant; that he was neither an indentured servant nor an apprentice (and so already bound by law to a master); and that neither was he ruptured, lame nor troubled with fits. Recruiting officers were also solemnly warned against enlisting 'Strollers, Vagabonds, Tinkers, Chimney Sweepers, Colliers, or Saylors'. The first three categories were generally regarded as undesirable characters, and chimney sweeps and colliers were considered with good reason

The 1742 *Cloathing Book* must be used with care as a source for 1745–46. The large cuffs that it shows being worn by Blakeney's 27th Foot (left) had most likely given way to a more conventional style by 1745. (Right) Ligonier's 59th Foot are depicted in the *Cloathing Book* with – erroneously – no lace. Despite its relatively high number this unit escaped disbandment at the end of the war, to become the 48th Foot.

to be prone to respiratory diseases, while any sailors enlisted in the Army were obviously lost to the fleet – and, given their notoriously roving nature, were perhaps also regarded as particularly susceptible to desertion.

Enlistment was supposedly for life, but, while there are a few instances of genuinely old men in the ranks – such as John Tovey of the 37th, who was 'born in the army' and all of 59 years old when he had his jaw shot away at Culloden – most were discharged in their 40s. Since the established strength of a regiment was usually halved following the conclusion of hostilities, it was easy enough for a soldier to obtain his discharge at that point if he desired it. If he was reckoned to be of good character he might be recommended to a Chelsea Out Pension, on the surprisingly frequent grounds of being 'worn out'.

Additional Companies

When a battalion of the Line was ordered overseas a rudimentary depot would be left behind for recruiting purposes, normally comprising a handful of officers and NCOs. Since such a small party was clearly inadequate to service a battalion on active service in wartime, in June 1744 two so-called Additional Companies were added to the establishment of each regiment serving in Flanders, and were authorized to be up to 100 strong. Ordinarily the function of these Additional Companies was no more than the intensive recruiting and basic training of men for their parent units, but at the outset of the Jacobite emergency all of the English-based holding companies were hastily formed into provisional battalions, and placed under the command of field officers of Marines. Thus, on 13 September 1745, the Additional Companies of the 3rd, 19th, 31st, 33rd and 37th Foot were ordered to be formed into a provisional battalion under Col Robert Frazer of the 2nd Marines; those of the 4th, 11th, 13th, 28th, 32nd and 34th Foot were ordered to be formed into a second provisional battalion under LtCol Duncombe of the 8th Marines; while those of the 8th, 12th,

The neatly schematized illustrations from the *Cloathing Book* and Morier's paintings have formed a popular image of the British redcoat of the 1740s, but in the field his appearance was often rather different. These shabby and burdened figures sketched from life by the 'Penicuik artist' in Edinburgh early in 1746 are in fact British regulars as they really looked on campaign; note the uncocked hats and unhooked coat-skirts, the knapsacks and canteens, and the casually carried muskets.

20th, 23rd, 36th and 59th formed a third unit under John Cotterell of the 6th Marines. All three battalions were employed on garrison duties: Frazer's at Newcastle upon Tyne, and the other two at Portsmouth and Plymouth respectively. The nine Scots-based Additional Companies had a rather more adventurous time. Those of the 1st (Royals) were ordered to reinforce the garrison of Fort William, but were captured by the Jacobites en route. Those of the 21st and 25th ended up in Dumbarton and Stirling Castles respectively. One of the Black Watch companies was lost at Prestonpans, and one served with Loudoun in the north; the third – Campbell of Inverewe's – fought at Falkirk and at Culloden.

'Vestry men'

At the same time, with the ordinary recruiting service completely disrupted by the emergency, two other sources of recruits were tapped. In the previous year the government had already passed an Act (18 Geo.II, c12) enjoining magistrates and parish constables to deliver up 'all such able-bodied, idle, and disorderly persons who cannot upon examination prove themselves to exercise and industriously follow some lawful trade or employment'. Popular legend notwithstanding, the 18th-century Army was not some sort of ambulant penal institution; recruiting officers were normally instructed to be very particular about the class of men they enlisted, requiring that they be 'of good character', and regularly declining the kind invitations of magistrates to empty the local gaols. These 'Vestry Men' (so-called because a bounty of £3 was paid into the local vestry fund to provide for any dependents which they might leave as a burden on the parish) were therefore just the type of recruit which regiments normally avoided. It is not surprising that those swept up in the first draft were assigned to Phillips' 40th Foot in the remote garrisons of Newfoundland, only for more than half of them to be lost in the wreck of the *Tyger* in February 1745. Subsequent drafts were then hurriedly parcelled out amongst the regiments returning from Flanders to deal with the Jacobite emergency, and it is clear from the surviving documentation that they were effectively assigned by those regiments to low-grade tasks such as battlefield clearance, burial details and prisoner-handling, afterwards being discharged at the earliest possible opportunity.

Prisoners of war

Rather ironically, some of those prisoners whom the Vestry men no doubt abused were then recruited to take their place. Ordinarily the enlistment of 'foreigners' was frowned upon, but as early as September 1744 the 39th Foot, stationed at Portsmouth, was authorized to take on Protestants from amongst the Polish prisoners of war then held in nearby Portchester Castle. In July 1746 no fewer than 250 rebel prisoners were allocated to the 38th Foot on Antigua, 100 more to the 63rd on Jamaica, and 200 each to the 65th and 66th Foot serving on Cape Breton Island in Nova Scotia. That these were not isolated incidents is confirmed by the subsequent enlistment in June 1747 of some Swiss prisoners of war, again allocated to the 39th Foot, and by the authorization in the same month of 12 Independent Companies to be raised largely from Jacobite prisoners, for a projected secret expedition to India.[1]

PROVINCIALS AND VOLUNTEERS

English 'Noblemens' Regiments'

Soon after the outbreak of the Rising, various noblemen enthusiastically offered to raise and maintain volunteer corps, but as the true cost of doing so became apparent they soon clamoured for their regiments to be accepted as regulars and thus paid for by the Crown. At first sight this request might not seem unreasonable, but the sticking point was the appointment of the officers. Only 49 out of a total of 475 officers in 15 regiments were already holders of the King's commission, and while a further 28 were retired officers or taken from the half-pay list, the vast majority had nothing to recommend them but the patronage of their noble sponsors. As temporary volunteers this would not have mattered; but taking their regiments into the Line would secure for them permanent commissions, on exactly the same footing as professional soldiers who had spent many years rising to their present ranks. Both Parliament and the Army accordingly objected, both to the immediate injustice, and to the inevitable prospect of accommodating a large influx of undeserving appointees to the half-pay list (indeed, two of these officers would still be drawing half-pay as late as 1798). However, in the circumstances there seemed little alternative, and after the King's personal intervention they were reluctantly, albeit briefly, taken into the Line as the 9th and 10th Horse and the 67th to 79th Regiments of Foot.

Even then it took some time before the new units were fit for any kind of service. The Duke of Bedford's Regiment was reported 'half compleat' and officially taken into the Line as the 68th Foot on 10 October 1745; but three weeks later a thoroughly unhappy Duke of Cumberland reported that 'I am sorry to speak my fears that they will rather be a hindrance than a service to me, for this regiment was represented to be the most forward regiment of them, yet neither officers nor men know what they are about, so how they will do before an enemy God alone knows'.

---

1 This was Admiral Boscawen's attempt to capture Pondicherry from the French. One of the Jacobite prisoners recruited for these companies, James Miller, left an interesting account of their experiences.

Front, rear and side views of a grenadier cap of Earl Harcourt's 76th Foot. It has a bright yellow front with a red 'bag' at the rear. Ordinarily this would indicate that the regiment wore red faced with yellow. The frontal embroidery includes a crown, a peacock resting in a coronet between green branches, and on the 'little flap' a trophy of red and green banners. The yellow rear band shows a central red diamond shape, between red flowers and fruit on branches with small white birds. (Courtesy Andrew Cormack)

These Noblemens' Regiments were mainly employed as garrison troops (neither Falmouth's nor Edgecumbe's Regiments ever left Cornwall) or, as in the case of Montagu's Ordnance Regiment, to guard rebel prisoners. In short, they were – in the 18th-century expression – a 'job', or corrupt trick. Their real purpose was to demonstrate the patriotic credentials of their sponsors, while unlocking access to all the customary allowances and 'emoluments' attaching to the command of a regiment, with little of the attendant trouble and expense incurred by professional soldiers. The exception was the Duke of Kingston's 10th Horse, who found themselves assigned to Cumberland's blocking force in the Midlands and (no doubt to the surprise of all concerned) proved surprisingly useful. Their good showing may have been because, as a newly raised unit, they were less constrained by old-established tactical doctrines that saw regular dragoons employed as battle cavalry rather than as scouts and skirmishers. Consequently, Cumberland took something of a fancy to them, and when they were officially disbanded he had them taken into the Line as the (albeit short-lived) 15th Dragoons.

English volunteer units

In addition to these battalion-sized creations there were also a number of local volunteer units, such as a company of gentlemen in London who proclaimed themselves the Loyal Blue Fusiliers; the more famous Yorkshire Blues are illustrated in Plate E2. Such companies were naturally of very limited use as conventional military units, but some of them, such as the eight companies of Col Graham's Liverpool Blues, played a vital second-line role; they assisted with the transportation of supplies, broke down the Mersey bridges, and latterly helped to garrison Chester. A cavalry unit, variously known as the Royal Hunters or Yorkshire Hunters, took part in the ultimately fruitless attempt to prevent the rebel army escaping back to Scotland late in 1745. With those exceptions aside, the ordinary policing tasks undertaken by these units – such as searching for arms and arresting 'suspected persons' – may not have been particularly glamorous, but the availability of volunteers freed precious regular troops from diversion to such tasks.

The same might also be said with some justice of the county militias. As an organization the Militia was all but moribund in 1745. The court martial of LtCol Durand, the unfortunate Guards officer assigned to defend Carlisle, evidenced a host of failings in the Cumberland Militia, who were reluctant to muster, poorly armed, totally untrained and hopelessly undisciplined. Nevertheless, what was overlooked – both by the court, and by generations of historians entertained by their antics – is that this sorry crew did in fact manage to hold the city and delay the Jacobites for a whole week, with quite incalculable consequences on what followed.

Scottish units

By contrast, the Scottish provincial and volunteer units generally had a less formal standing than their English counterparts, but saw a good deal more service.

The earliest was the Edinburgh Regiment, properly authorized by formal Letters of Service on 9 September 1745, and 200 strong within the week. The better part of them were involved, together with the old soldiers of the Edinburgh City Guard, in Gardiner's abortive attempt to block the Jacobite advance at Corstophine on 15 September. Afterwards, when the city fell, some may have swelled the garrison of the Castle, while about 80 joined Cope just before Prestonpans. Effectively that should have been the end of them; but on 20 November they were reconstituted by LtGen Roger Handasyde (under the patronage of the Earl of Hopetoun), and formed the nucleus of a whole brigade of loyalist volunteers. This also included a small battalion of 180 men from Paisley and Renfrew under the Earl of Glencairn; another of about 400 raised in Stirling and Linlithgow; and no fewer than 15 companies of the Glasgow Regiment under the Earl of Home, a Scots Guards officer who also had command of the whole brigade. With the exception of the Edinburgh Regiment these units were raised on the local authority of the then acting commander-in-chief Scotland, Gen Handasyde, and did not enjoy the same quasi-regular status as the 'noblemens' regiments'. Yet for all that some of them fought stoutly enough at Falkirk, and 19 widows of Glasgow men killed there would receive money from the charitable Guildhall Fund.

In addition, as in England, considerable numbers of volunteers were raised for local defence:

John Campbell, Younger of Mamore (1723–1806), commanded the Argyleshire Men at Culloden – see Plate D2. 'Colonel Jack' later had the great good fortune of succeeding to the dukedom of Argyle as the 5th Duke, after the 3rd Duke died childless in 1761 and the title passed to the Mamore line.

> *Pursuant to a recommendation by the Lord Justice Clerk, lists of able-bodied men proper to be intrusted with arms had been made up by the heritors of several counties, with the assistance of the parish ministers. A small corps of them accordingly came into town [Edinburgh] on the 30th [December] and a considerable number in a day or two after. Several ministers marched with their parishioners, some of them in arms. The volunteers of the associate congregations of Edinburgh and Dalkeith, seceders from the established church, kept in a body by themselves, and had proper colours, with this inscription* – For Religion, the Covenants, King and Kingdoms. *Their ministers did not march with them. All had arms and ammunition delivered them out of the King's magazine in the castle.*

Two Scots loyalist volunteers sketched by the 'Penicuik artist' in Edinburgh. It was clearly cold that day – one has his hand stuffed in his pocket, and the other has a greatcoat draped over his shoulders. Judging by this artist's treatment of similar figures, the man on the left would appear to have a belly-box strapped around his waist.

Similarly situated were the Argyle Militia, and the various Highland Independent Companies. At the end of October 1745, MajGen John Campbell of Mamore was instructed to go to Inverary and there raise 'eight Independent Companies each of 100 men with the proper officers; and likewise to arm 16 such companies more, without the charge of commissioned officers, who are to serve without pay and are to be raised from the Duke of Argyle's and the Earl of Breadalbane's Contrays'. A combination of administrative obstruction and bad weather delayed Mamore's actual arrival there until 22 December, but in the meantime his son LtCol 'Jack' Campbell of the 64th Highlanders had set to with a will; he led 12 of the companies to Falkirk, together with three of his own regiment and Inverewe's Black Watch company. For the most part thereafter

they were employed on what were effectively anti-partisan operations, but 'Colonel Jack' famously led the four regular companies and four of the best Argyle companies at Culloden.

Nor were these the only Highlanders to serve King George. Back in September 1745, Cope had left a company of the 64th and the depleted remnants of a Black Watch company at Inverness. When the Earl of Loudoun came north they too formed the nucleus of a small loyalist brigade of 18 independent companies, raised under the authority of the Lord President, Duncan Forbes of Culloden.

FOREIGN TROOPS

The Dutch

Aside from the 16-strong troop of Hungarians and Germans who formed the Duke of Cumberland's personal bodyguard, there were two major foreign contingents serving alongside the British army during the campaign. The first was Dutch, provided under a treaty of mutual assistance between Great Britain and the United Provinces, which obliged each to come to the aid of the other in case of threatened or actual invasion. The previous year a Dutch contingent had already spent some time in England in anticipation of a French invasion that never came. They had returned to Holland in June 1744, but in response to the actual Jacobite emergency in 1745 a fresh contingent was demanded. Unfortunately the situation in Flanders was equally precarious, as the French steadily exploited their victory at Fontenoy in May, and the only regiments that could be spared were those that had been paroled after the surrender of Tournai, on condition of not fighting against the French army or its allies for 12 months.

Commanded by Prinz Moritz of Nassau, who apparently still considered himself under a cloud after rendering up the fortress, and by MajGen Carol Diederik Schwanenburg, the contingent comprised five Dutch regiments – Braekel, Holstein-Gottorp, Tissot van Patot, Villattes, and La Rocque, each of two battalions – and a Swiss regiment, Hirtzel, with three battalions, together with a contingent of artillerymen but no cavalry. Some of the Dutch units were originally landed in the Thames near London, but eventually all were concentrated at Newcastle upon Tyne, where they formed a major part of Field Marshal Wade's army. The Dutch regiments appear to have been quite weak; originally reckoned to be 9,000 strong at the commencement of the siege of Tournai, only 5,300 men had marched out on 9 June. Allowing for artillery and other ancillary personnel, this would imply an average strength of just under 400 men per battalion, although there are indications that the three Swiss battalions may have been stronger than their Dutch counterparts.

Initially they were welcomed, especially at Berwick, where one of the battalions of the Regiment La Rocque stiffened the rather lonely garrison of 5 companies of Lee's 55th Foot. However, once the novelty wore off they soon began to be compared unfavourably with British troops, though opinion was divided as to whether the Dutch or Swiss were worse. In part this was due to their poor physical condition; they lacked shoes, and initially even horses for the general officers, let alone any more substantial logistic support. Consequently, they were soon being accused of robbery, riot and affray; they were also blamed for a quite understandable lack of enthusiasm when Wade's attempted march across the Pennines foundered in deep snow at Hexham. Sickness was also rife amongst them, and by 11 December they were down to just 2,500 effectives.

Ultimately, however, a far more serious problem was their legal status. From the very beginning the French government had protested about their employment against the Jacobites, especially as by the Treaty of Fontainbleu on 5 November 1745 the rebels were formally declared to be French auxiliaries. In early December, when Lord John Drummond arrived in Scotland at the head of a small French expeditionary force, one of his first acts was to send a letter to Nassau demanding the immediate withdrawal of the Dutch contingent. At first Nassau and Schwanenberg were inclined to disregard the French demands, or at least (as Schwanenberg offered) to continue serving as garrison troops at Newcastle upon Tyne; but in the end it was decided to honour the letter of their parole terms and send the Dutch home – in the same ships that brought their replacements, a contingent of Hessian troops.

The Hessians

Hesse-Kassel was a German principality whose relatively large army was subsidized by periodically hiring out a number of units to neighbouring states such as Hanover, which in turn offset the cost with British gold. This apparent misappropriation of public funds to support the King's German patrimony had not been popular in Britain, and the imminent withdrawal of the Dutch contingent meant that it was both politically and militarily expedient to divert the Hessian troops to Scotland, even though this would weaken yet further the already overstretched Allied forces in Flanders.

It was at first hoped to bring over a balanced force of some 4,800 infantry and 1,200 cavalry under the Duke of Cumberland's brother-in-law, the Erbprinz (hereditary prince) of Hesse-Kassel, Friedrich Wilhelm. However, it was quickly realized that there was insufficient shipping available for all the horses, and in the end only a single squadron of 98 hussars were sent to Scotland. The infantry contingent was rather more substantial: the regiments Garde (with 833 men), Prinz Maximilian (829), Mansbach (836), Von Donop (833), Erbprinz (907), and the Grenadiere Regiment (830), totalling 5,068 men. The whole force was hired at a cost of 100,000 crowns, with an indemnity of 30 crowns to be paid for each infantryman discharged dead and 80 crowns for each cavalryman lost; there was also a stipulation that they were not to be employed as marines or in the colonies.

The terms having been agreed, the troops were embarked at Williamstadt and landed at Leith, the port of Edinburgh, on 10 February 1746. There they made a very good impression on observers, and Lord Mark Kerr considered them 'really fine troops, well appointed and clean'. Nevertheless, Cumberland himself seems to have been reluctant to employ them, hoping that by now he could settle the matter with British

This young fellow is identified as a Penicuick volunteer, but his relatively smart and soldierly appearance suggests that he had volunteered into the Edinburgh Regiment, the only complete provincial corps to be raised in Scotland – see reconstruction, Plate E3.

troops alone. For a time he was keen to send them straight back to Flanders, but he soon changed his mind.

His intention was to march his army around the east coast by way of Aberdeen, and this raised the uncomfortable possibility that while he was thus engaged the rebels might again 'attempt to slip into the Lowlands', as they had done the previous September. Accordingly, the Hessians were reinforced by a cavalry brigade comprising St George's 8th Dragoons, Naizon's 13th and Hamilton's 14th Dragoons, and moved up to Perth in order to cover against this possibility. A localized Jacobite offensive did in fact take place in March; a number of small government listening posts were seized, and Blair Castle was besieged. Cumberland, by then at Aberdeen, was keen that the Hessians should relieve the place, and impatient when the Erbprinz proved reluctant to force the Pass of Killiecrankie.

Relations between the two then took a further turn for the worse when a Hessian hussar officer was captured in a skirmish near Pitlochry, and was promptly released with a letter proposing that a cartel be arranged for the exchange of prisoners. As such an arrangement was common in continental warfare at the time the Erbprinz was happy to agree, but Cumberland – only too well aware of the political implications – flatly refused. Unfortunately the Erbprinz had a keen sense of his own importance and, as even Frederick the Great was moved to comment, 'precedence is all he thinks about'. He declared that without such a cartel he would not move north of Perth; consequently, the Hessians took no further part in the hostilities, and on 20 May 1746 they were ordered home by way of Newcastle upon Tyne.

The 'Penicuik artist's' charmingly characterful sketch of two Hessian officers in Edinburgh – see reconstruction, Plate H2.

(continued on page 33)

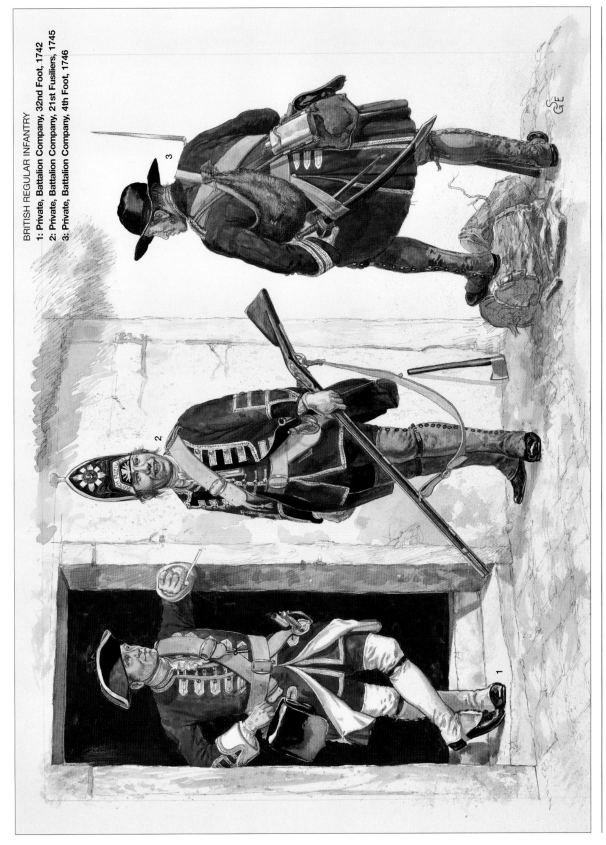

BRITISH REGULAR INFANTRY
1: Private, Battalion Company, 32nd Foot, 1742
2: Private, Battalion Company, 21st Fusiliers, 1745
3: Private, Battalion Company, 4th Foot, 1746

A

1: Trooper, 13th Dragoons
2: Invalid
3: Private, 9th Marines

B

1: Cadet, Royal Artillery
2: Drummer, Royal Artillery
3: Staff officer

C

HIGHLAND INFANTRY
1: Private, 43rd Highlanders (Black Watch)
2: Field officer, 64th Highlanders
3: Highlander, Independent Company

D

PROVINCIAL INFANTRY
1: Grenadier, Granby's 71st Foot
2: Private, Yorkshire Blues
3: Private, Edinburgh Regiment

E

CAVALRY
1: Trooper, 10th (Kingston's) Light Horse
2: Trooper, Duke of Cumberland's Hussars
3: Trooper, Georgia Rangers

F

DUTCH AUXILIARIES
1: Private, Zwitzersch Infanterie Regiment Hirtzel
2: Dutch artilleryman
3: Private, Infanterie Regiment Villattes

G

HESSIAN AUXILIARIES
1: Grenadier, Grenadiere Regiment
2: Hessian officer
3: Trooper, Husaren Korps

H

THE REGIMENTS

Abbreviations: 'D. of', 'E. of', 'M. of', 'Vis', 'Ld' = Duke, Earl, Marquis, Viscount, Lord.

Life Guards
All in red coats with blue facings, buff waistcoats and breeches, and gold lace.

Troop	Colonel*	Remarks
1st Life Guards	Earl De La Warre	
2nd Life Guards	Lord Cadogan	
3rd Life Guards	Lord Tyrawley	disb. Dec 1746
4th (Scots) Horse Guards	Earl of Crawford	disb. Dec 1746
1st Horse Grenadier Guards	Richard Onslow	caps
2nd Horse Grenadier Guards	Earl of Rothes	caps

(* Commanding officers as at 19 Aug 1745)

Horse
Apart from the Royal Horse Guards (Blues), who still ranked at this period as the 1st Horse, all regiments of horse and dragoons were in red coats with facing-coloured waistcoats and breeches.

Seniority	Colonel	Facings	Remarks
Royal Horse Guards	D. of Somerset	blue coats faced red	('Blues')
2nd (King's)	Honeywood	blue	1st KDG 1746
3rd (Queens)	D. of Montagu	buff	2nd QDG 1746
4th	Wade	white	3rd DG 1746
5th	Browne	blue	1st Irish 1746
6th	Wentworth	green	2nd Irish 1746
7th	Bowles	yellow	3rd Irish 1746
8th	Sir John Ligonier	black, buff lining	4th Irish 1746

Dragoons

Seniority	Colonel	Facings	Remarks
1st (Royal)	Hawley	blue	
2nd (R. North British)	E. of Stair	blue	caps
3rd (King's)	Bland	light blue	
4th	Rich	green	
5th (Royal Irish)	Molesworth	blue	
6th (Inniskilling)	E. of Rothes	yellow	
7th (Queen's)	Cope	white	
8th	St George	orange	
9th	de Grangues	buff	
10th	Cobham	yellow	
11th	Kerr	white	
13th	Gardiner/F. Ligonier	green	
14th	Hamilton	buff	

1st Horse Grenadier Guards, as depicted in the 1742 *Cloathing Book*. This was one of two troops of dragoons attached to the Household Cavalry, and served during the campaign with the army covering London.

ABOVE LEFT

This elaborately embroidered grenadier cap has previously been identified as belonging to an officer of the 2nd Dragoons (Scots Greys), but is actually that of an officer of the 2nd (Scots) Troop of Horse Grenadier Guards, as evidenced by the Garter star on the main front and the thistle on the flap. The Greys, by contrast, had the star of St Andrew and the customary white horse of Hanover, respectively.

ABOVE RIGHT

At this period the mounted infantry heritage of Dragoon units was emphasized by the continued employment of drummers, carrying side drums at their saddle-bow and wearing caps such as this one. Similar to those worn by infantry drummers, it is identified as belonging to a regiment of dragoons by the cavalry cornets embroidered on either side of the drum.

BELOW LEFT

Four troops of Ligonier's 8th Horse were with the army defending London, while two troops accompanied Cumberland north to Carlisle. This surviving cornet, said to have been carried at Dettingen two years earlier, is crimson with gold and silver embroidery. It provides a good example of the way in which commanding officers were still prone to placing their own arms on standards – in this case those of Sir John, later Lord Ligonier.

BELOW RIGHT

Guidon of Rich's 4th Dragoons, *c.*1742; like Ligonier's regiment, it still bears the Colonel's arms – a practice officially forbidden in 1743 but probably persisting for some time afterwards.

Foot

All regiments in red coats, waistcoats and breeches, except Footguards and Royal regiments, who were allowed blue breeches, and the two Highland regiments in plaids.

Seniority	Colonel	Facings	Remarks
1st Footguards	D. of Cumberland	blue	
2nd Footguards	E. of Albemarle	blue	
3rd Footguards	E. of Dunmore	blue	
1st (Royals)	St Clair	blue	2 bns
2nd	Kirke	sea green	
3rd (Buffs)	Thos. Howard	buff	
4th	Barrell	blue	
5th	Irwin	gosling green	
6th	Guise	yellow	
7th Fusiliers	Hargrave	blue	caps
8th	Ed. Wolfe	blue	
9th	Reade	yellow ochre	
10th	Columbine	bright yellow	
11th	Sowle	green	
12th	Skelton	yellow	
13th	Pulteney	philemot yellow	
14th	Price	buff	
15th	Harrison	yellow	
16th	Rich. Handasyde	yellow	
17th	Tyrell	white	
18th	Mordaunt	blue	
19th	Chas. Howard	yellowish green	
20th	Bligh/Sackville	pale yellow	
21st Fusiliers	Campbell	blue	caps
22nd	O'Farrell	pale buff	
23rd Fusiliers	Huske	blue	caps
24th	Houghton	willow green	
25th	Sempill	yellow	
26th	Anstruther	pale yellow	
27th	Blakeney	buff	
28th	Bragg	yellow	
29th	Fuller	yellow	
30th	Frampton	pale yellow	
31st	Hy. Beauclerck	buff	
32nd Fusiliers	Douglas	white	
33rd	Johnson	red	
34th	Cholmondley	bright yellow	
35th	Otway	orange	
36th	Fleming	green	
37th	Monro/Dejean	yellow	
38th	Dalyell	yellow	
39th	Richbell	green	
40th	Phillips	buff	
41st (Invalids)	Wardour	blue	

42nd (disb. 1748)	Oglethorpe	green	
43rd Highlanders 42nd Hldrs 1748	Ld Jo. Murray	buff	
44th (1st Marines) (disb. 1748)	Churchill	yellow	
45th (2nd Marines) (disb. 1748)	Fraser	green	
46th (3rd Marines) (disb. 1748)	Holmes	yellow	
47th (4th Marines) (disb. 1748)	Torrington	white	
48th (5th Marines) (disb. 1748)	Cochrane	pale yellow	
49th (6th Marines) (disb. 1748)	Laforey	green	
50th (7th Marines) (disb. 1748)	Cornwall	white	
51st (8th Marines) (disb. 1748)	Jordan	yellow	
52nd (9th Marines) (disb. 1748)	Poulett	philemot yellow	
53rd (10th Marines) (disb. 1748)	Agnew	yellow	
54th (43rd Foot, 1748)	Graham	white	
55th (44th Foot, 1748)	Lee	yellow ochre	
56th (45th Foot, 1748)	Warburton	deep green	
57th (46th Foot, 1748)	Tho. Murray	yellow	
58th (47th Foot, 1748)	Lascelles	white	
59th (48th Foot, 1748)	F. Ligonier/Conway	buff	
60th (disb. 1748)	Bruce	black, white linings	
61st (disb. 1748)	Folliot	white	
62nd (disb. 1748)	Battereau	yellow	
63rd (49th Foot, 1748)	Trelawney	green	
64th Highlanders (disb. 1748)	Loudoun	white	
65th (disb. 1748)	Shirley	green	American
66th (disb. 1748)	Pepperell	green	American

ABOVE LEFT
The old-fashioned single-breasted coat worn by the 20th Foot in this figure from the 1742 *Cloathing Book* had been superseded by the usual lapelled design by the time of the Rising – compare with Plate A1.

ABOVE RIGHT
In 1742 the 25th Foot was still known – confusingly – as the Edinburgh Regiment. In 1745–46, Sempill's 25th Foot included a significant number of Scots officers and soldiers, and one its few casualties at Culloden was a man named John MacDonald.

LEFT
One of the famous 'Mutinier' prints depicting some of those involved in the Black Watch mutiny of 1743, providing a crude but useful image of one of the 43rd Regiment's pipers. The significance of the red cross on the yellow or buff pipe-banner is uncertain.

Provincial regiments

Most in blue, faced with red; see commentaries, Plates E1 and F1.

Regiment	Colonel	'half compleat'	disbanded
9th Horse	D. of Montagu	22 Oct 1745	early Aug 1746
10th Horse	E. of Kingston	12 Oct 1745	15 Sept 1746
67th Foot	D. of Bolton	15 Nov 1745	13 June 1746
68th Foot	D. of Bedford	10 Oct 1745	late Aug 1746
69th Foot	D. of Montagu	22 Oct 1745	early Aug 1746
70th Foot	D. of Ancaster	1 Nov 1745	16 June 1746
71st Foot	M. of Granby	4 Nov 1745	late Aug 1746
72nd Foot	E. of Berkeley	23 Nov 1745	26 June 1746
73rd Foot	E. of Cholmondley	4 Nov 1745	20 June 1746
74th Foot	E. of Halifax	18 Oct 1745	early Aug 1746
75th Foot	Vis. Falmouth	2 Nov 1745	late June 1746?
76th Foot	E. Harcourt	13 Nov 1745	17 June 1746
77th Foot	E. Gower	22 Oct 1745	17 June 1746
78th Foot	Herbert	8 Nov 1745	late June 1746?
79th Foot	Edgecumbe	3 Dec 1745	late June 1746?

(Also included should be the Edinburgh Regiment, granted Letters of Service on 9 September 1745, but never taken into the Line and so not numbered.)

Edinburgh Volunteers (left) by the 'Penicuik artist'; the full-bottomed wig suggests that they belonged to a militia rather than to the provincial Edinburgh Regiment.
(Right) Two unhappy-looking volunteers of the Edinburgh City Watch, depicted standing guard at one of the capital's gates. Note the sword hilt protruding through a slit in the heavy caped watchcoat.

PLATE COMMENTARIES

A: BRITISH REGULAR INFANTRY

The uniforms worn by British regular infantry during the '45 are relatively well recorded, but accurate interpretation of those records is confused by a number of factors. The primary source is generally regarded as the comprehensive series of illustrations comprising the 1742 *Cloathing Book*, which for the first time recorded – though apparently none too faithfully – the facings, lace patterns and occasional idiosyncrasies of the uniforms worn by every regiment in the Army.

It did not, of course, record those regiments raised after 1742, and it is also known that a number of alterations were made to the styling of some uniforms before 1745. For example, the 20th Foot, who fought at Culloden as Bligh's Regiment, were depicted in 1742 wearing single-breasted coats, but on 17 November 1743 it was ordered that 'all the coats of the infantry be lappeled that are not so already, and that all be made with the same sort of pocket as the Scotch Fuziliers, viz., in the plaits of the coat'. There were also alterations to some of the cuff styles, and – just as importantly – alterations in the way the uniform was actually worn.

Furthermore, in order to properly display all details of the individual uniforms the *Cloathing Book* depicted both lapels and coat skirts fully fastened back; but there is ample evidence to show that normally the skirts were worn unhooked, and in cold or wet weather (as during much of the Jacobite campaign) the lapels were fastened across. Conversely, in warmer weather the waist belt was increasingly coming to be worn under the coat rather than over it as depicted in 1742, perhaps responding to contemporary continental fashions. As these figures show, the *Cloathing Book* must therefore be used with caution.

A1: Private, Battalion Company, 32nd Foot, 1742

William Douglas's 32nd Foot was based in and around London during the Jacobite campaign, but its precise status is unclear. Oddly enough, some of the Marching Order books in WO5 refer to the unit as Fusiliers, and this title may be borne out by the fact that in the 1740 *Army List* its junior subalterns were designated as second lieutenants rather than as ensigns. On the other hand, the *Cloathing Book* depicts ordinary hats rather than caps, and the presence of second lieutenants may simply be a reflection of the fact that the regiment were originally raised as marines. This soldier is representative of the oldest style of clothing and equipment depicted in the *Cloathing Book*, and is noteworthy for the unfashionable single-breasted coat abolished in 1743.

A2: Private, Battalion Company, 21st Fusiliers, 1745

Sir James Campbell's Royal Scots Fusiliers had a surprisingly broad role in the campaign. At the outset two Additional Companies were recruiting at Glasgow and subsequently formed part of the garrison of Dumbarton Castle. The service companies returned from Flanders to serve under Cumberland in his march north to Carlisle, and so missed fighting at Falkirk. Subsequently at least one company under LtCol Sir Andrew Agnew went north to occupy Blair Castle, while another under the rather elderly Capt John Crosbie (first commissioned 1 March 1704, and a captain since 25 March 1724) garrisoned Aberdeen. The

remaining eight companies of the regiment led by Major the Hon Charles Colvill fought at Culloden, afterwards returning just seven men wounded.

This soldier, based in large part upon the image of a fusilier in the *Cloathing Book* and on studies of the Footguards by Paul Sandby dated 1745, illustrates the difference in appearance resulting from moving the waist belt inside the coat and throwing back the unhooked skirts. Blue breeches were a distinction peculiar to Royal regiments, and most infantrymen wore red like the soldier of the 32nd. As a fusilier rather than a grenadier he lacks the brass match case customarily attached to the cartridge box sling.

Also of interest is the fusilier cap. Both David Morier's later painting of c.1748 and the Royal warrant of 1751 give the grenadier company a blue-fronted cap bearing a thistle on red within a crowned circle or collar of St Andrew (green edged in yellow with 'Nemo Me Impune Lacessit' embroidered in yellow). However, the *Cloathing Book* shows that the battalion or fusilier company men wore a slightly different cap, as here. The green collar was displayed on a star of St Andrew, and, while the grenadier had the customary white horse of Hanover and motto 'Nec Aspera Terrent' placed on the 'little flap', this fusilier has a thistle in place of the horse and the regimental title in place of the motto. The title according to the *Cloathing Book* was 'Royal Fuziliers', but this is almost certainly a mistake: the same basic engraving was used for all three fusilier regiments, and

Fusilier of the 21st Foot, as shown in the 1742 *Cloathing Book* – see Plate A2.

David Morier's 'Incident of the Rebellion' is undoubtedly the most famous near-contemporary image of British troops in action, but is also surprisingly problematic – see commentary to Plate A3. Simply referred to in the inventory of Cumberland's paintings made in 1765 as 'A Skirmish between some Highlanders and English Infantry', it is presumed to depict Barrell's 4th Foot at Culloden. As the evidence suggests that it was painted in the early 1750s, the 'Highlanders' may well have been other members of the 4th Foot suitably disguised, rather than Jacobite prisoners – as fancifully claimed by Lord Frederick Campbell in the 19th century. (The Royal Collection © 2012 Her Majesty Queen Elizabeth II/The Bridgeman Art Library)

the title seems to have been carelessly carried over from the 7th Royal Fusiliers. Contemporary usage, including the order cited above, would suggest that the title embroidered on the cap was actually 'Scotch Fuziliers'.

A3: Private, Battalion Company, 4th Foot, 1746

William Barrell's 4th Foot returned from Flanders to serve creditably under Hawley at Falkirk, and famously bore the brunt of the fighting on the left wing at Culloden, losing 17 officers and men killed and 108 wounded, out of 373 present and fit for duty that morning.

The figure usefully provides a very good example of the difficulties of establishing exactly what was really worn by regiments in the '45, and is primarily reconstructed from contemporary sketches by the so-called 'Penicuik artist' of British soldiers passing through Edinburgh. The outline is straightforward and emphasises the practical and comfortable nature of the ordinary soldier's uniform as worn on campaign, with the coat skirts unhooked and the hat slouched in an unmilitary manner. However, ascertaining some of the detail of that uniform is surprisingly problematic, with no fewer than three sources available for this particular regiment: the 1742 *Cloathing Book*, David Morier's series of grenadier paintings from *c*.1748, and the same artist's famous 'Incident of the Rebellion', presumed to depict Barrell's Regiment at Culloden.

The first source is slightly problematic not only in its early date, but also in the fact that the illustration re-used the same base engraving as for the 2nd Footguards. This may explain why the coat pockets are depicted as vertical with a herringbone lace pattern exactly as for the Coldstreams, while Morier's 1748 painting – although otherwise consistent – shows a more conventional horizontal pocket, but omits the lace edging to the skirts shown in 1742. However, the very fact that the Coldstream engraving was re-used rather than another may indicate that this was indeed the arrangement used by the 4th Foot. Apart from the lace pattern itself – plain white for the Coldstreamers, and a blue worm for Barrell's – the only other real differences between the two regiments appear to be the absence of a badge on the cartouche box for Barrell's, and the arrangement of the lace on the cuffs. On the whole, both the 1742 and 1748 depictions of the uniform are consistent (albeit the pocket style must have changed in 1743), but this is not true of the Culloden painting. That shows a slightly different shape of cuff, slightly narrower lapels, a very different style of grenadier's wings, and – most striking of all – a herringbone lace pattern on the sleeve in place of the ladder pattern depicted in both 1742 and 1748. All of this tends to support a possible later date of some time in 1750s for the Culloden painting – which was also, as it happens, the only period when the 4th were quartered near London, and thus convenient for Morier's studio.

B1: Trooper, 13th Dragoons

Colonel James Gardiner's 13th Dragoons was one of two regular cavalry regiments to serve at Prestonpans, where Gardiner himself was mortally wounded. Both regiments had earlier spent a prolonged period of garrison duty in Ireland, and in the months leading up to the Rising were 'at grass' – i.e. the horses were being pastured to fatten them up for the winter, while the troopers undertook the dismounted phase of their annual training cycle. With their horses suffering from sore backs, neither the 13th nor Hamilton's 14th Dragoons were regarded as properly fit for service, and their defeat at

Prestonpans evidently left them completely demoralized. Their subsequent performance did not much improve; the 13th, by then under Col Francis Ligonier, served with scant distinction at Falkirk, while their comrades of the 14th Dragoons ran away at the very outset of the battle, riding over the unlucky Glasgow Volunteers.

This figure is partially based on the relevant illustration from the *Cloathing Book* and partly on a surviving coat found in Edinburgh, which differs in minor details. Whilst lacking the facing-colour lapels of infantry uniforms, the coat was nevertheless double-breasted and could be fastened over in bad weather. Long boots and the styling of the coat aside, the most obvious difference between cavalry and infantry uniforms was that the former wore facing-coloured waistcoats and breeches – in this case green – rather than red. This was because cavalry uniforms were issued on a two-year cycle, and the troopers were therefore not expected to turn their old coats into waistcoats as in the infantry.

This trooper's equipment reflects his original role as a mounted infantryman, in which he was still trained – and indeed as some other units performed for what was probably the last time at Clifton Moor on 18 December 1745. As a cavalryman he carried a basket-hilted broadsword and had a pair of pistols in saddle-holsters, but as a mounted infantryman he would also carry a firelock, bayonet and cartouche box. The firelock was officially designated a carbine, but for dragoons it was of the same calibre as infantry muskets and had a 42in barrel – the same length as the later Short Land Pattern firelock of 1768.

B2: Invalid
Soldiers disabled by old age, wounds or other infirmities but still willing and able to serve could apply to be posted to the various Independent Companies of Invalids scattered around the British Isles, doing garrison duty at the more substantial fixed military establishments, or acting as caretakers and storekeepers in smaller ones, such as Ruthven Barracks in the Highlands. Thus when Sgt Terry Molloy, left in charge of that post, was summoned to surrender to the rebels in August

1745, he answered that he 'would take his chance' despite his garrison comprising just 12 men 'whereof three were useless'. Given that the Invalids quite literally included the halt, the lame and the partially blind, that may not have been too uncharitable a description. (Molloy was not himself an Invalid, but served in the ranks of either Guise's 6th Foot or Lee's 55th. He was rewarded for his bravery by being commissioned a lieutenant in the latter regiment.) At Carlisle the two Independent Companies were the mainstay of the defence, and when the Militia finally refused to fight Col Durand decided that he could no longer hold out as 'we remained with only our few Invalids, who from their great age and infirmities, and from the excessive fatigue they had undergone … were rendered in a manner of no use.'

Our reconstruction is based on both the 1742 *Cloathing Book* and Morier's painting of c.1748, neither of which show any material difference in the uniform. The only difference between the two depictions is that in the former the Invalid carries his ammunition in a belly-box, while in the latter he has the full infantry equipment depicted here. Presumably it varied according to the differing duties of the various companies and detachments – and the immediate situation. When occupying a fixed position there was generally no occasion for the wearing of marching gaiters, and most illustrations show the men wearing stockings and shoes only.

B3: Private, 9th Marines
The marine regiments raised in 1739 and 1740 were originally Army units intended for seaborne operations in the Caribbean; therefore, although identified as the 1st to 10th Marines, they took precedence in the Army List as the 44th to 53rd Foot. The effective abandonment of operations in that theatre after the disastrous Carthagena operation meant that they were gradually scattered throughout the fleet by companies and detachments without regard to their original organization – to the frustration and dismay of those subsequently responsible for the impossible task of sorting out their finances. In the end their accounts were not cleared until 30 October 1764 – fully 16 years after the last were disbanded. In the meantime, as there was no requirement for field officers of marines to serve at sea, they were instead employed on special service. The provisional battalions formed from Additional Companies were commanded by marine officers; for example, LtCol Charles Whitefoord of the 5th Marines served both on Gen Cope's staff at Prestonpans and afterwards as a volunteer at Culloden. Ordinary marines also took part in the campaign, both on board ship in naval actions against blockade runners and ashore. Captain John Gore's company of the 9th Marines were landed from HMS *Gloucester* in order to secure the burgh of Montrose ahead of Cumberland's advance in February 1746.

Representing all of them, this reconstruction of one Capt Gore's men is distinguished by his 'philemot yellow' facings – a brownish shade, likened to that of dead leaves. Once again, the only real source for their uniforms is the 1742 *Cloathing Book*, and the usual uncertainty as to the degree of change that may have taken place by 1746 is compounded by the administrative confusion which surrounded the marine units. One of the problems, as an anguished Board of General Officers reported in January 1746, was that the clerks on men-of-war were failing to distinguish the regiments to which the marines assigned to them belonged. 'hereby cutting off all means of tracing them forwards or backwards'.

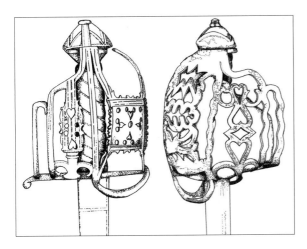

(Left) The classic Glasgow-style broadsword hilt was favoured not only by most Highland officers, but also by many cavalry units. (Right) The rather freer Stirling-style hilt was less popular in military units, but was favoured by some officers of the Black Watch.

Consequently there is no certainty that any alterations in the style of the uniform filtered through to all of the men, and, given the ships' clerks failure to identify the different regiments to which they belonged, there is obviously some doubt as to whether an individual soldier serving at sea would even receive the correct uniform for his own corps. All that can be said with any certainty is that when they passed into Admiralty control in 1747 the problem was solved by ordering that all ten regiments were to wear red coats 'breasted in the lapel fashion, face turned up with bright yellow, white metal buttons, good Kersey breeches, stockings, shoes etc'. Very properly, the marines were also then to have 'A cap with an anchor and cable embroidered on the front'.

The choice of a cap as the ordinary headgear from their very first raising no doubt arose from the practical consideration that it could be jammed on to the soldier's head far more securely than an ordinary cocked hat, and for similar reasons their personal equipment was confined to a belly-box and pouch on a waist belt and a bayonet but no sword. The latter would obviously be an encumbrance on board ship, and no doubt if one was required they could draw an ordinary naval cutlass. Another concession to their nautical environment was that while soldiers serving in regiments of the Line were accustomed to burnishing the barrels of their firelocks with all manner of abrasive substances (to the frequently expressed dismay of the Ordnance Office), Sea-Service weapons were normally painted black as a protection against corrosion.

C1: Cadet, Royal Artillery

Officers of the Royal Artillery had in effect to serve an apprenticeship, which from 1741 comprised theoretical work as Cadets at the Royal Military Academy and practical experience as lieutenant fireworkers. In the company present at Culloden, Capt-Lt John Godwin had a lieutenant and two second lieutenants serving under him, and no fewer than five lieutenant fireworkers. Technically the officers and men of the Royal Artillery were not part of the British Army but answered to the Board of Ordnance, and this independence was demonstrated in their uniforms, which only broadly conformed to Army garments in style and were completely different in colour. Instead of red coats they wore blue, and had different conventions as to how the red facing colour was displayed, as seen here.

Again, the available evidence is problematic, but this reconstruction is based on a watercolour sketch added to the copy of the *Cloathing Book* held in the library at Woolwich, which presumably dates from around 1742. It shows unlaced blue lapels, while a large group painting by Morier depicting officers and men of the Royal Artillery at Roermond in 1748 shows red lapels. Both paintings show the scarlet waistcoat and breeches, but the earlier watercolour shows the coat skirts hooked back. Taken together with the fact of his carrying a fusil and cartouche box, this suggests that our subject is a cadet rather than a commissioned officer, which might also explain the blue lapels.

C2: Drummer, Royal Artillery

The rank-and-file of the Royal Artillery also wore blue coats faced with red, but were distinguished from officers by having blue waistcoats and breeches, though there is some

Cadet, Royal Artillery, after a 1742 watercolour – see discussion in commentary to Plate C1.

uncertainty as to exactly what was worn in 1745. Another watercolour sketch in the library at Woolwich shows quite a plain blue coat lined and cuffed in red, with red half-lapels, and yellow lace only on the sleeve buttonholes and in chevrons on the coat skirts like the cadet. Morier's Roermond painting. on the other hand, adds considerably more yellow trimming to full-length lapels, to the cuffs and to the waistcoat. Exactly when this changeover occurred is unclear, but it probably took place some time after 1743, and may have lagged behind the alterations in the infantry uniform, to judge by a 1769 minute which belatedly noted that 'His Majesty has given certain regulations [in 1768] for the cloathing of the several marching Regiments which may occasion some small alterations in the cloathing of the Royal Artillery'.

Three drummers – Thomas Dixon, George Guthrie and Francis Naylor – served with Godwin's company at Culloden, and this reconstruction is based on a slightly indistinct figure in the Roermond painting. In broad outline the style is very similar to that of infantry drummers with the exception of the cap, which appears to be slightly taller and more pointed in shape like a grenadier cap rather than a normal drummer's cap. Although it has no tuft at the top it presumably has the usual falling bag – in this case blue rather than red. Both front and frontlet are red, with the usual scrollwork embroidery in yellow. The main device is the arms of the Ordnance Office: a fairly squat blue shield bearing three cannon one above the other in silver, and a white or silver chief with three black or dark blue cannonballs set side by side in a row. The frontlet has no lettering, just a very fat bombshell with golden flames.

C3: Staff officer

There was at this time no prescribed uniform for officers serving on the staff, who therefore wore pretty much what they pleased. This might be their ordinary regimentals, which were themselves unregulated except by custom and practice. For formal occasions, including portraits, coats

Facsimile of the famous sketch of James Wolfe made by George Townshend at Quebec in 1759. Despite the date, the uniform shown is of interest as an example of the rather plain 'frock suits' worn by officers on active service – see staff officer in Plate C3.

two of them properly clothed, armed and fit for service. The third, commanded by Aeneas Mackintosh, the Laird of Mackintosh, was still awaiting its arms, but as it had been raised in the Inverness area Cope elected to take it with him on his march north, together with Sir Patrick Murray of Ochtertyre's Perthshire company. Both suffered badly from desertion, and while a remnant of Mackintosh's company was left at Inverness, Ochtertyre's, assigned to guard the baggage at Prestonpans, was taken prisoner there. The remaining company, commanded by Capt Duncan Campbell of Inverawe, was sent to Inverary to form the nucleus of what became known as the Argyleshire Men, and so not only escaped the debacle but saw considerable service, culminating in its fighting at Culloden under its second-in-command, Dugald Campbell of Auchrossan.

Again, our reconstruction is substantially based on the image of a soldier of the regiment in the 1742 *Cloathing Book,* with the customary reservations as to its applicability in 1745. A very noticeable feature depicted in the *Cloathing Book* is the double-breasted jacket very like a cut-down dragoon coat, with buttons set back from the edge on both sides, and cavalry-style cuffs but no lapels. However, slightly later illustrations – such as the well-known prints depicting the three ringleaders of the Black Watch mutiny of 1743, and Johan Christian Leopold's sketches of Highland soldiers in Germany – appear to show single-breasted jackets. Nevertheless, as it is possible that these were depicted wearing their waistcoats, the 1742 pattern jacket is shown here. The famous belted plaid was not a substitute for breeches, but rather a large cloak kilted up above the knees, which at once made the jacket superfluous in warm weather and was something of an encumbrance when not required. At home Highlanders were wont to discard it and go about in their long shirt tails, and as a compromise this soldier (following Leopold) has let the upper part of his plaid hang

were cut from fine quality scarlet cloth of a much brighter colour than those worn by the rank-and-file, with facings of similar quality, while gold or silver lace replaced the worsted trimmings worn by the men. Such coats were obviously expensive; while Charles Parquin's commanding officer in Napoleon's army famously declared that an officer cannot be too well dressed in the presence of the enemy, British officers (and soldiers) have always taken a more practical attitude.

The costume worn by this officer – in his own way as shabby as the soldier of Barrell's in A3 – is partly based on a well-known 1759 watercolour sketch of James Wolfe (who served on Gen Hawley's staff during the Culloden campaign), though with features more suitable for the 1740s; these include the use of a tied-back wig. He wears what was referred to as a 'frock suit' in plain red without any regimental distinctions. In 1749 LtCol Samuel Bagshawe estimated the cost of a frock suit to be half that of laced regimentals, and in 1768 Capt Thomas Simes recommended that on being first commissioned a young officer should obtain two frock suits. Aside from its everyday practicality and comparative cheapness, another advantage of the frock suit was that since it displayed no regimental distinctions it could be worn through successive transfers from one unit to another. In Wolfe's case the large and old-fashioned cuffs sketched by Townshend in 1759 clearly show that his coat was not specifically run up for the North American campaign, but one of his old frocks from his days as a junior regimental officer in the 1740s. About the only indication of this gentleman's status as a staff officer rather than a regimental officer is the fact that he wears a substantial pair of riding boots.

D: HIGHLAND INFANTRY

D1: Private, 43rd Highlanders (Black Watch)
The three Additional Companies of the Black Watch recruiting in Scotland at the outbreak of the Rising were reckoned by Sir John Cope to be 'pretty near compleat', and

Soldier of the 43rd Highlanders, after the 1742 *Cloathing Book* – see Plate D1. Other than the obvious fact of the jacket being shorter, note its similarity in cut to the dragoon style at the chest and cuffs.

Grenadier cap, Granby's 71st Foot, with a blue front and a red 'bag' at the rear – see Plate E1. The dark blue rear band bears a red diamond shape, and leafy branches of what appear to be red roses. (Courtesy Andrew Cormack)

down at the rear. In time the obvious next step of stitching part of an old plaid into a kilt without this upper part would be taken – and almost certainly originated within the Army's Highland regiments in order to preserve a proper military appearance.

In this case the tartan is the original one used for the Black Watch companies when they were regimented to form the 43rd Foot in 1739. After his appointment as colonel of the regiment in April 1745, Lord John Murray introduced a red overstripe to the sett. The actual date when this occurred is unknown, but it is unlikely to have taken place before the Rising.

D2: Field officer, 64th Highlanders

This reconstruction is partly based on a later Thomas Gainsborough portrait of the leader of the Argyleshire Men, 'Colonel Jack' Campbell, as well as on a contemporary portrait of his commanding officer, John Campbell, Earl of Loudoun. The fine quality scarlet jacket with white facings is unremarkable except inasmuch as a portrait of another officer of the 64th, Lt John Reid of Straloch, shows a single-breasted garment, as do portraits of junior officers in other Highland regiments raised in the 1750s. This might suggest that lapels may at this time have been confined to field officers' jackets. The waistcoat, interestingly, appears to be of the same tartan as the plaid, albeit more finely woven with smaller checks.

The tartan worn by this regiment does raise an interesting question. In Loudoun's portrait it is unquestionably red, and has been identified as the sett now known as Murray of Tullibardine. Although no plaid is visible in Reid's portrait, his red tartan waistcoat appears to corroborate this. However, in the Loudoun papers there is some correspondence from August 1746 relating to the provision of plaids for the regiment and this, tantalisingly, includes actual samples of the material for soldiers'- and sergeants'-quality plaids. Essentially these appear to be of the government or 'Black Watch' sett with the addition of a red and a yellow overstripe (just as the later Highland Light Infantry and Seaforths added a red and a white overstripe). It is unclear, however, whether this was the original tartan worn by the regiment, or whether both the 43rd and the 64th added the overstripes to the government sett at the same time in order to distinguish themselves one from the other, and perhaps also from the Highland Independent companies raised during the Rising. That does not, of course, account for the red tartans

apparently worn by the officers, but the most likely explanation is that at this early period those gentlemen either pleased themselves as to what tartan they chose to wear, or, at best, agreed amongst themselves on a suitable sett rather than taking the common government one. It may be significant that whilst 'modern' Campbell tartans are based on the Black Watch sett, many contemporary portraits of Campbell gentlemen show them favouring red.

D3: Highlander, Independent Company

Young Mamore's Highland battalion is popularly known as the Argyle Militia, but in official returns it was rather more accurately referred to simply as the Argyleshire Men, reflecting the fact that at Culloden the battalion actually comprised four companies of regulars from the 43rd and 64th Highlanders and four Highland Independent Companies, all of them raised in or around the county of Argyle.

While accounted as regulars rather than as militia, there is no evidence that these or the other Highland Independent Companies received any uniform clothing until after the fighting was over, when red jackets faced with yellow were issued together with plaids, presumably of the government or 'Black Watch' sett. In the meantime this obviously raised the issue of how to distinguish them from the otherwise identically clad highlanders marching in the rebel ranks, and in the immediate aftermath of the debacle at Falkirk the suggestion was actually made that they be issued with soldiers' three-cornered hats. Had this eccentric suggestion been followed up they would indeed have been easily recognized – but instead, each man was given a red cross to attach to his bonnet. This was obviously much easier to distinguish at a distance than a black cockade. A Jacobite account of the abortive attempt by Locheil to rally the clans at Invermallie in May 1746 tells us that it was hastily abandoned when some scouts he sent to investigate a body of approaching highlanders reported they 'were certainly Loudoun's, for they saw the red crosses in their bonnets'. It is uncertain what form these red crosses took, but they are not to be confused with the unknown badges, marked with each man's number, identifying members of the original Highland watch.

While there is evidence that Mamore was at some pains to secure broadswords as well as firelocks for his Argyleshire men, Loudoun's Independent Companies were rather less well provided for. As was rather irritably pointed out, the loyal clans had earlier surrendered or otherwise disposed of their arms in conformity with the law, and particular mention is made of the fact that the Independent Companies under Macleod who were defeated at Inverurie on 23 December 1745 lacked 'their darling weapon, the Broadsword'.

E: PROVINCIAL INFANTRY

E1: Grenadier, Granby's 71st Foot

Lord Granby's Foot, originally sponsored by his father John Manners, 3rd Duke of Rutland, was a typical provincial 'Nobleman's Regiment', reported 'half compleat' and accordingly taken into the Line on 4 November 1745. At the time the ten companies were widely scattered, with six at Leicester, two at Loughborough and two at Harborough; but once accepted they were ordered to concentrate, first at Nottingham on 12 November and afterwards at either Litchfield or Warwick. At that stage they were still being positioned to counter the Jacobite threat to London, but after the Pretender's forces turned back from Derby they were ordered to Newcastle upon Tyne on 9 January, and would remain there for the rest of the campaign, replacing some of the Dutch troops ordered home after the intervention of the French. On 27 June 1746 they were ordered back to Leicester, and disbanded there in the second half of August.

Despite being numbered as regular regiments of the Line, most of the provincial corps appear to have been dressed in blue rather than red coats. This was certainly true of Lord Herbert of Cherbury's 78th Foot, and this reconstruction of the 71st is based in part on a portrait of the young Lord Granby in a blue uniform faced red (of a quite different style to that of the Blues with whom he served later in his career), and a surviving grenadier cap of the regiment. In Granby's case the waistcoat was also red, but as with the Royal Artillery this may well have been a distinction of officers' uniforms; as depicted here, both waistcoats and breeches normally followed the coat colour for the rank-and-file of infantry units.

On the other hand, a second surviving grenadier cap, from Harcourt's 76th Foot (see page 20), features what was originally a very bright yellow front, indicating that this regiment – which undertook various garrison duties in southern England – had red coats faced with yellow. Equally, Berkley's 72nd had red faced with green, and Gower's 77th were also redcoats.

E2: Private, Yorkshire Blues
Equally typical of the Volunteer units were the Yorkshire Blues. Their origins lay in a patriotic association of the principal nobility, gentry, and clergy of the county, formed at York on 23 September 1745, which raised £31,420 'for the support of the Government and the defence of the county'. The money funded four companies of infantry, each of 70 men exclusive of sergeants, corporals, and drummers. Designated as the Yorkshire Blues, they remained embodied for about four months; the officers served without pay, the sergeants receiving 14 shillings per week, the drummers 10 shillings and the privates 7 shillings.

Their title derived obviously enough from their uniform, which for the West Riding companies comprised double-breasted coats of blue korsey faced with red kersey, with baize lining and 24 buttons to a coat. The clothing for the East Riding companies was described as 'exactly the same as the Swiss and Dutch troops are clothed, but with the linings considerably better'. From the low allowance of buttons and the fact that the Swiss at least had no lapels (see Plate G2), it may safely be conjectured that the Yorkshire Blues wore fairly simple uniforms similar in cut to those subsequently adopted by the Norfolk Militia, as depicted here.

One of the officers, Capt William Thornton of Thornville Royal, proposed that they should serve alongside the regular army like the Noblemen's Regiments. When this suggestion was rejected, he went and recruited an independent company of his own and 'sent immediately to Leeds for cloth of a good quality for their cloathing. The coats were blue, trimmed and faced with buff, [with] buff waistcoats'. Presumably the alteration in the facing colour was intended to distinguish his volunteers, who were attached to Pulteney's 13th Foot at Falkirk, from the original Yorkshire Blues. Tradition has Thornton (and the company fiddler, 'Blind Jack' Metcalf of Knaresborough) following the army all the way to Culloden, but in fact it appears that he and his men returned home after Falkirk as a result of a dispute over billeting.

Private, Norfolk Militia, 1758, depicted in a plain red coat with dark blue collar and cuffs, a red waistcoat, and russet-coloured coat lining and breeches. At the time of the Rising militia units had no uniforms, but, while dating from more than a decade later, this illustration provides a useful example of the simple style of uniform probably adopted in 1745 by local volunteer units such as the Yorkshire Blues – see Plate E2.

(Incidentally, the volunteers raised in Devon were reportedly given blue coats lined and faced with red, hats edged with white worsted lace, and a pair of white gaiters to each man. Whether they also received waistcoats and breeches or had to make do with their own is not recorded.)

E3: Private, Edinburgh Regiment
This provincial regiment originally received its letters of service on 9 September 1745 and, with a brief hiatus during the Jacobite occupation of the capital, spent most of its existence on garrison duty there. However, a detachment did serve at Prestonpans, and another at Falkirk. As provincials, they are not to be confused either with the various small units of Edinburgh Volunteers, or the Edinburgh City Guard, a paramilitary police force largely made up of former soldiers that had long kept order in the city.

The three companies of the Guard had red uniforms faced with blue, but otherwise there appears to be no information available as to any uniforms that may have been worn by Lowland Scottish units recruited during the Rising. It is possible that the Edinburgh Regiment, as a properly constituted provincial corps, may have worn the dark blue coats with red facings adopted by two successive regiments of Edinburgh Volunteers – the credit of the capital may have demanded nothing less – but there is no direct evidence.

This stalwart looking figure is therefore based on a contemporary sketch labelled a 'Penicuik Volunteer' – perhaps one of the Midlothian fencibles brought into Edinburgh from the outlying parishes in the first week of January 1746. As depicted in the original he has only a black cockade, belly-box and firelock to mark him as a volunteer, although some of the Presbyterian Seceders may have worn the old Protestant blue ribbon instead, just as they carried at least one colour from the Army of the Covenant of a century before – a blue flag with five red roses in the centre of a white saltire on a blue ground, bearing the old inscription 'For Religion, the Covenants, King and Kingdoms', which is still preserved in the National Museum of Scotland.

F: CAVALRY

F1: Trooper, 10th (Kingston's) Light Horse

In addition to the provincial regiments of foot, two cavalry regiments were also temporarily taken into the Line: the Duke of Montague's 9th Horse (not to be confused with his regular 7th Horse), and the Duke of Kingston's 10th Horse. The latter fought at Culloden, and initially escaped disbandment by being taken into the Line as the 15th Dragoons, before being disbanded after all in 1748.

As with the other provincial regiments, information on the uniforms worn by these units is scanty, and in this case is confused by a David Morier painting of the then 15th Dragoons immediately prior to their disbandment in 1748, which unsurprisingly depicts a dragoon-style uniform. Our reconstruction is instead based on an *Ipswich Journal* account of men being raised for Montague's 9th Horse, whose 'clothing [is] to be Blue lin'd red, and yellow buttons'. As this is consistent with what little is known of the other temporary provincial and volunteer corps there is no reason to suppose that Kingston's Horse wore red prior to their conversion to dragoons. Another, albeit slightly oblique clue is provided by an odd incident a few days before Culloden, when an unknown rebel officer reportedly stripped some prisoners of their coats in order to clothe his own men. Ordinarily, dressing rebel soldiers in red coats would have made no sense, but blue coats taken from the 31 men of Kingston's captured in the affair at Keith on 20 March 1746 might have been a different matter.

Otherwise the uniform and equipment is of the usual pattern for regiments of horse, with narrow lapels extending the full length of the coat. The buff waistcoat and breeches are speculative, partly based on the 15th Dragoons painting which shows buff rather than the then-green facing colour, and partly on the probable need to make a distinction from the uniform of the 1st Horse (Blues), who had red waistcoats and breeches. Writing some 30 years later in 1778, Thomas Hinde claimed in his *Discipline of Light Horse* that Kingston's Horse were intended to imitate the hussars in foreign service, and that 'Their accoutrements were as light as possible of every sort and species. Their arms were short bullet guns or carbines, shorter than those of regiments of Horse and slung by their sides by a moveable swivel to run up their shoulder belt; their pistols upon the same plan, as they used both carbines and pistols on horse-back, indiscriminately. Their swords were very sharp and inclined to curve'. Given the haste with which the regiment was raised during the Jacobite emergency this description is as unlikely as it is beguiling, and there is no other evidence for such non-regulation arms being procured at this time. Instead, therefore, our subject is conventionally equipped with a broadsword and a 36in-barrel carbine fully stocked to the muzzle, like those then carried by other regiments of horse.

Interestingly, very similar descriptions are given of Oglethorpe's volunteer Yorkshire Hunters, or Royal Hunters, who were 'all dress'd in Blue, trimm'd with Scarlet, and Gold buttons, Gold lac'd hats, Light boots and Saddles &c. their Arms were short Bullet Guns slung, Pistols of a moderate size, and strong plain Swords' All were supposedly gentlemen, but we are told that their servants, who made up the second and third ranks, had to make do with brass rather than gilt buttons. Another description adds the curious detail that they wore green cockades in their hats, presumably as a compliment to Oglethorpe, whose own regiments had green facings.

F2: Trooper, Duke of Cumberland's Hussars

General officers were customarily accompanied by a number of troopers serving as orderlies and escort. Such men were normally drawn on a temporary basis from the ranks of a convenient regiment of horse or dragoons, but the Duke of Cumberland – as befitting his unique status as a prince of the blood and son to the Elector of Hanover – had a permanent bodyguard of Hussars. These were effectively Hanoverian household troops, and as such the only true Hanoverian soldiers to serve in the campaign. There are few references to the unit during the Rising; but they were certainly at Clifton, where 'one of the Duke's Hussars', identified as an Austrian, captured a Jacobite hussar (Capt John Hamilton of Redhouse), and some 16 of them were also at Culloden. Fortunately their uniform is recorded in the background to two paintings of Cumberland by Paul Sandby, which both show a dark green dolman and pelisse, and crimson waistcoat and breeches – Cumberland's livery colours. In outline the uniform could be said to follow the classic hussar styling, although the comparatively heavy boots are unusual.

F3: Trooper, Georgia Rangers

Looking equally out of place in this campaign were the Georgia Rangers. Brigadier General James Oglethorpe was simultaneously Governor of the colony of Georgia and colonel of both the then-42nd Foot, a regular regiment of the Line specifically raised as its standing garrison, and of a

Trooper, Royal Horse Guards (The Blues), 1742. Until the raising of the provincial and volunteer units in 1745 this regiment, ranked as the 1st Horse, was unique in wearing blue coats rather than red. In order to avoid close imitation, it is likely that the two provincial cavalry regiments had buff waistcoats and breeches rather than the red shown here – see Plate F3, Kingston's Light Horse.

regular provincial corps of Georgia Rangers, which initially comprised one company of Highlanders and another of Boatmen. In 1745 he was in England recruiting an augmentation to the Rangers in the form of two mounted troops, whose intended role was to serve as cavalry, patrolling the Georgia coast. These each had an establishment of one captain, two lieutenants, a cornet, four quartermasters, two French horns and 60 private men – very similar to that of the troops of light dragoons added to regular units in 1756. The two troops were actually embarked for America at Hull, only to be quickly brought ashore again and assigned to Field Marshal Wade's army. Brigaded with a volunteer regiment of horse variously known as the Yorkshire Hunters or Royal Hunters (who to the confusion of historians also placed themselves under Oglethorpe's command), they subsequently crossed the Pennines to join Cumberland's army. They fought in the series of skirmishes culminating in the action at Clifton on the evening of 18 December.

The only description of their appearance comes from a Jacobite officer who referred to them being 'clo'ed in green with leather caps', and this reconstruction is therefore in part based on the style of clothing later to be adopted by light dragoons – with the exception of the leather cap, here modelled after a very practical style originally known as a Montero, apparently worn by other American Ranger units and even by a proposed corps of military artificers. Just what the Jacobites may have made of the most exotic member of the corps, referred to in contemporary newspaper accounts as an 'Indian King' – presumably one of Oglethorpe's Creek allies – can only be guessed.

G: DUTCH AUXILIARIES

The Dutch contingent, led by Count Moritz van Nassau and MajGen Carol Diederik Schwanenburg, comprised six infantry regiments – those of Hirtzel (Swiss), Braekel, Holstein-Gottorp, Tissot van Patot, Villattes and La Rocque – supported by a small train of artillery.

G1: Grenadier, Zwitzersch Infanterie Regiment Hirtzol

This reluctant member of Marshal Wade's forces is based on one of the few Dutch Army figures included in David Morier's series of paintings of grenadiers serving with the Allies in the Low Countries in 1748. Swiss units of the Dutch Army, including that of Gen Saloman Hirtzel von Wolflingen, were immediately distinguishable from Netherlands and German ones by the wearing of dark blue rather than straw-coloured waistcoats, and by an absence of lapels, but otherwise they followed the same basic style and colouring.

G2: Dutch artilleryman

Dutch gunners at this period wore a very traditional uniform comprising a dark blue coat faced with red, red small-clothes and brass buttons. While the Dutch contingent arrived at a critical time and formed a very substantial part of Wade's army operating in the North-East of England, it would appear that a little party of just nine artillerymen sent across to participate in Cumberland's siege of Carlisle were the only Dutch troops to actually see any action before being shipped home again due to the intervention of French troops (thus justifying this gunner's burn injuries).

G3: Private, Infanterie Regiment Villattes

Unfortunately, for some reason only a very few Dutch troops were included in Morier's paintings of the Allied forces in 1748, and this reconstruction of a soldier serving in one of Nassau's regiments is therefore partially based on a Morier painting depicting Independent Companies. That provides a good idea of the general cut of the uniform and style of hat, while the regimental distinctions are taken from a near contemporary schematic. With the exception of the Swiss and the three red-coated regiments of the Scots Brigade (who still carried British colours at this period), all Dutch infantry units – such as this one commanded by MajGen Henri des Villattes – wore dark blue coats with red facings, straw-coloured waistcoats, blue breeches and white buttons. Regimental distinctions were largely confined to the presence or absence of lapels, the arrangement of the lace (if any) and buttons on the coat, and the colouring of the *Trodel* or sword-knot . Belly-boxes appear to have been worn by all Dutch infantry, and were not confined to grenadiers or auxiliary units as in the British service.

H: HESSIAN AUXILIARIES

H1: Grenadier, Grenadiere Regiment

Included in the Hessian contingent was the Grenadiere Regiment, originally formed in 1697 as a composite battalion drawn from six regimental grenadier companies, and formally reconstituted as a permanent unit in 1702. As such it gained its own colours, but all six companies of the regiment continued to wear grenadier caps, which by 1746 had assumed the tall tin-fronted style favoured by most North German states. The extravagant whiskers seen here are taken directly from one of David Morier's paintings; since they are significantly larger than those sported by other Hessian grenadiers, they may be a regimental affectation.

H2: Hessian officer

While the Dutch had spent the campaign in northern England, the Hessians went directly to Scotland, where – socially, at least – they found themselves welcome, perhaps because their behaviour was very correct and quite uninfluenced by any partisan sympathies. The Lowland Scots and German tongues sound surprisingly similar, and while officers no doubt got by well enough in French when mixing with Edinburgh society, it was reported that in Perthshire Hessian officers found it easiest to converse with their landlords in Latin.

This Hessian officer is directly copied from one of the Penicuik sketches, evidently made on a cold day; he wears an undress *Rock* or frock-coat over his regimentals and is keeping his hands warm with a fur muff. The same artist also sketched the children 'playing at Hessians'.

H3: Trooper, Husaren Korps

The Husaren Korps accompanying the Hessian contingent had been raised for reconnaissance duties as recently as 1744, as a single squadron of two companies, and as depicted here was dressed in what was already the traditional style. Not all of them were *bona fide* Hungarians, and the captured officer whose release led to the row between Cumberland and the Erbprinz was identified in contemporary accounts as a Swede. (This is not as surprising as it might at first appear, since the Landgraf of Hesse-Kassell was himself the younger brother of the King of Sweden, and the two states were effectively ruled by the latter – in similar fashion to King George's possession of both Great Britain and Hanover.)

INDEX